Fifth Avenue Sermons

Fifth Avenue SERMONS

BY

J. Sutherland Bonnell

Harper & Brothers Publishers
New York 1936 London

FIFTH AVENUE SERMONS

Printed in the United States of America

FIRST EDITION

L-L

To

BESSIE CARRUTHERS BONNELL

my wife

this book is

affectionately dedicated

*

CONTENTS

Acknowledgments

The author wishes to express his appreciation to the following authors and publishers for their generous permission to quote from their copyrighted works:

To the Clarke & Stuart Co., Limited, Vancouver, B. C., and the author, F. G. Scott, C.M.G., D.S.O., for the poem, "The Heaven of Love."

To Chapman and Hall, Ltd., London, England, for quotation from *Religion and Communism* by Julius F. Hecker, Ph.D.

To Harcourt, Brace and Company, Inc., for "The Watcher-Mother" from *Cross Currents* by Margaret Widdemer; for quotations from *Modern Man in Search of a Soul* by C. G. Jung, and *The Microbe Hunters* by Paul de Kruif.

To The Macmillan Company for quotations from "St. Paul" by F. W. H. Myers; "The Everlasting Mercy" by John Masefield, and "The Trial of Jesus" by John Masefield.

To John Oxenham for the use of his poem, "A High Way and a Low."

To Harper & Brothers for quotations from *The Holy Bible: A New Translation* by James Moffatt; *A Gentleman in Prison* by Tokichi Ishii, and *Man the Unknown* by Alexis Carrel.

To Houghton Mifflin Company for quotation from "The Ancient Sage" by Alfred Tennyson.

To Robert M. McBride & Company for quotation from *Psychology and Morals* by J. A. Hadfield.

To Fleming H. Revell Company for quotation from *The Romance of Preaching* by Rev. Sylvester Horne.

Fifth Avenue Sermons

IS THE UNIVERSE FRIENDLY TO MAN?

Are not two sparrows sold for a farthing? and one of them shall not fall on the ground without your Father . . . Fear ye not therefore, ye are of more value than many sparrows.

MATTHEW 10:29 and 31

AN INTERESTING story has been told of the friendship of Matthew Arnold, the English poet and critic, and F. W. H. Myers, the philosopher and spiritualist. They had been conversing about man's place in the universe, when suddenly Arnold turned to Myers and asked, "If you were permitted to ask one question of the Sphinx, with the assurance that a correct answer would be given, what question would you ask?" After a moment's reflection Myers replied, "I should ask, 'Is the universe friendly?' "

Whether this anecdote be true or not I cannot say. Frankly, I have my doubts about many of these tag ends of biography. The fact remains, nevertheless, that it would be difficult to suggest a problem more fundamental than that which was involved in the question ascribed to Myers—"Is the universe friendly?"

Human destiny hangs upon the true answer to that query. If you and I were to concentrate our thought upon a certain set of facts: the vastness of the universe and its apparent indifference to the fate of man, its hostility and its harshness, we might well answer the question in the negative. Oftentimes pestilence lays its gaunt hand upon whole populations. Volcanoes pour forth molten lava, overwhelming crowded villages and towns as thoughtlessly as a man might pour a kettle of boiling water on an anthill. Earthquakes hurl men into eternity as a dog shakes off drops of water after a plunge into a lake. Who will aver that these things happen in a friendly universe?

Not a few among modern skeptics assure us that the universe is definitely hostile to man. "Humanity must continue to exist . . . upon sufferance in a universe not made for it," says one. "Man is a cosmic accident," says another. "Man is a disease on the surface of our planet, an eczema that will soon be cured," affirms a third. These modern writers but echo the plaint of Omar Khayyam when he says:

> 'Tis all a checker board of nights and days
> Where destiny with men for pieces plays.
> Hither and thither moves and mates and slays,
> And one by one back in the closet lays.

One reason for our bewilderment, of course, is that science has ushered us into a universe so boundless that our earth, in relation to the rest of creation, is comparable to a speck of dust floating around in St. Paul's Cathedral. Well might we utter the petition of the Breton fisherman: "God have mercy on us; thine ocean is so vast and our boat is so small."

In the midst of our perplexities, however, there are some reflections which steady us.

The first is a realization of the greatness of man himself.

On this planet, surrounded by flaming suns, trailing meteors, majestic constellations, there emerged this remarkable creature man. It was not long before he discovered in his own mind a key which unlocked for him the secrets of the universe. However hostile the forces of the cosmos may appear to be, man is gifted with powers that enable him to harness these forces to do his bidding. His restless mind is forever exploring the unfathomed spaces and charting the visible universe.

I stood one night in the observatory on the top of the Physics Building at Columbia University and looked at the heavens through the giant telescope there. For a long time I gazed at Betelgeuse in the constellation of Orion.

"That star you are looking at," said the astronomer quietly, "is many millions of times greater than our sun. About fourteen years ago we measured it with the interferometer. By means of the spectroscope we have analyzed its chemical constituents."

As I listened to him I looked away from the telescope through which I had been gazing at that distant point of light and turned in astonishment to look at something far more wonderful—the astronomer who stood before me. Betelgeuse, in spite of its immensity, was not even conscious of its own existence; but here was a man, riding on this ball of earth as it speeds through the sky, reaching out to distant stars, discovering the laws that govern them, analyzing the elements of which they are composed, weighing and measuring them one by one. The truth was borne in upon me that man's exploration of the universe has revealed to him nothing half so wonderful as his own personality.

Canon Scott, a Canadian poet, has put that thought into unforgettable verse:

> I rose at midnight and beheld the sky,
> Sown thick with stars like grains of golden sand
> Which God had scattered loosely from his hand
> Upon the floorways of his house on high.
> And straight I pictured to my spirit's eye
> The giant worlds, their course by wisdom planned,
> The weary waste, the gulfs no sight hath spanned,
> And endless time for ever passing by.
> Then filled with wonder and a secret dread
> I crept to where my child lay fast asleep,
> With chubby arm beneath his golden head.
> What cared I then for all the stars above?
> One little face shut out the boundless deep,
> One little heart revealed the heaven of love.

Go into the nursery tonight and look down at a tiny face snuggled on its pillow and you will see something infinitely more wonderful than all the starry heavens.

A second reflection which comforts us, in our confusion, is the greatness of Jesus.

Even as the universe produced man with all his godlike powers, so from out of the human race there sprang that most majestic of all personalities—Jesus Christ. As he moved among men, instinctively they felt that he was greater than they. As they drew nigh to him they became aware of the nearness of God. As they listened to his words they were conscious of the accents of the Eternal. As they witnessed his deeds they realized that here was not only the First among all men but one who had no second. The Soul of creation looked out through his eyes. No interpretation of the universe can possibly be true which is not able to account for him. A cosmos that can produce a personality who, in his understanding, his compassion, and his love towers above men of all generations as did Jesus, must have something Christlike at its heart.

To Jesus, then, we shall go with our question—Is the universe friendly? He answers our query with a decided affirmative. There is no dubiety or hesitancy in his response. The universe, he affirms, is friendly to man. This is the theme of the passage from which our text is taken. Jesus assures his disciples of God's unfailing protection. He points them to the humblest of Palestinian birds, little feathered creatures that were sold two for a farthing, and he declares that not one of these is forgotten of God. "Fear ye not therefore," he adds, "ye are of more value than many sparrows." Jesus never doubts that this world was brought into existence by God's creative activity and is sustained by his power.

Oftentimes he reasons from God's concern for his humbler creatures to his provision for man, the especial object of his love and care.

"Behold the fowls of the air: for they sow not neither do they reap, nor gather into barns; yet your heavenly Father feedeth them. *Are ye not much better than they?"*

"Consider the lilies of the field, how they grow; they toil not, neither do they spin: and yet I say unto you that even Solomon in all his glory was not arrayed like one of these. Wherefore if God so clothe the grass of the field, which today is and tomorrow is cast into the oven, *shall he not much more clothe you . . . ?*"

We cannot account for the faith of Jesus in God's unceasing care by declaring that he was a recluse who had deliberately fled away from the sufferings and trials that fall to the lot of man. The greater part of his ministry was spent in little Galilean towns, whose narrow, crooked streets were crowded with the lame, the palsied, the blind, and the diseased. They flocked to him as to a fountain of healing. Even those who were afflicted with loathsome leprosy found in him a friend. One of the most poignant verses in the New Testament reveals the extent of Jesus' ministry to the physically and mentally ill:

"Now when the sun was setting, all they that had any sick with divers diseases brought them unto him: and he laid his hands on every one of them, and healed them."

No Schopenhauer or Thomas Hardy ever looked half so deep into the abyss of human misery as did Jesus. Yet it was he who assures us that it is not the will of the Father that one of the least of his little ones should perish.

The clew to Jesus' faith in an unfailing Providence is found in his conception of God. When speaking of the fowls of the air he says: "Your heavenly Father feedeth them." Of the little sparrows he affirms: "One of them shall not fall on the ground without your Father . . ." Again when referring to man's physical requirements in food, drink, and clothing he declares:

"Your heavenly Father knoweth that ye have need of all these things."

We shall never be able to understand Jesus' teaching about God and man unless we remember that in all his thought of God, Fatherhood was central. Jesus held that the universe is friendly to man because it is the Father's world—the Father who paints the lilies of the field; who "stills the raven's clamorous nest"; who marks the flight of a sparrow; who watches over his human children with compassionate care, numbering the hairs of their head, loving them individually as though in his great family there were but one child to love.

This conception of God, the universe, and man as taught by Jesus is the basis of our faith in human brotherhood.

In the Sermon on the Mount, when he came to deal with human relations, he said: "Love your enemies, bless them that curse you, do good to them that hate you, and pray for them which despitefully use you and persecute you."

The all-sufficient reason, for Jesus, why men should so deal with each other, was this: "That ye may be the children of your Father which is in heaven."

The brotherhood of man is a teaching which it is easy to affirm but desperately difficult to practice. It is easy to stand in a Christian pulpit and preach about human brotherhood. It is easy to sit in a pew and nod a ready assent to this doctrine. But nothing short of the enthronement of the Spirit of Christ in our hearts will enable us to apply it in daily life.

I am aware of the fact that there are groups of people in the modern world who declare that they are now practicing human brotherhood and that they are doing it without regard to faith in God. They have outgrown the need of God, they assert. One of the frequent allegations of these people is that such a faith has made man socially lazy. He has put upon God's shoulders the tasks that he ought, himself, to have performed. He uses his religious beliefs as a means of escaping his bounden duty. We must build a social order, we are told, based on the principle of the brotherhood of man as laid down by the Carpenter of Nazareth. When we turn away from that vision to dogmatic affirmations about the Fatherhood of God and a friendly universe we are simply giving opium to the people.

But where, may I ask, in all the teaching of Jesus is there any explicit reference to the brotherhood of man? Not once did he use these words. They do not occur anywhere in the New Testament. The brotherhood of man is a doctrine of the Christian Faith not because it was explicitly taught by Jesus, but rather because it is an inescapable inference from his teaching of the Fatherhood of God. It is rooted and grounded in Jesus' conception of God, the universe, and man.

If what the skeptics say be true and man be only a beast that "nourishes a blind life within the brain"; if he be only a cosmic accident, a bit of organic scum, a disease on the planet that will soon be cured, what basis is there for believing in human brotherhood? Life becomes a struggle for existence around a jungle water hole. Who can blame the tiger because it leaps upon its victim? It is fulfilling its native instincts in killing for food. If man be no more than an animal, why should he not exploit, trample upon, and victimize his fellow creatures if it be to his advantage so to do? May he not, acting in this fashion, be fulfilling the highest law of his own being?

Unalterably opposed to such a conception of life and man stands the teaching of Jesus.

Only as we believe in God and in his Divine purposes have we the assurance that man is not a by-product flung off by a blind, mechanical universe: a creature whose ultimate destiny is annihilation—fated at the last to be "blown about the desert dust or sealed within the iron hills." Rather do we see him as he appeared to the eyes of Jesus—a child of God—an object of the Father's unwearying love and care. Only then, too, do we possess the assurance that there is a solution for all our problems and that the will of God one day will be performed on earth as it is now done in Heaven.

The present world situation with suspicion, hate, greed, and other fierce passions of the human heart flaming afresh might well drive us to despair were it not that, across the black clouds that lower over the world, there is a rainbow of hope—the over-arching Fatherhood of God with its promise of the ultimate realization of the brotherhood of man. This triumphant certainty must inspire the Church of Jesus Christ to renewed endeavor, not that it may identify itself with this or that social panacea or political platform, but rather that it shall become a voice of Judgment upon all injustice and oppression, upon all exploitation of man by man, upon all that cheapens life and debases human personality; holding ever before the minds and hearts of men the glorious vision of that better World Order that yet must come—the new society of the Kingdom of God on earth.

Another implication of Jesus' teaching about God, as set forth in our text, is that each of us has an individual claim upon him. The Father who watches over the sparrows will care for his children one by one. Jesus never wearied of emphasizing this fact. On one occasion he turned to the multitude and said: "What man is there of you whom if his son ask bread, will he give him a stone? or, if he ask a fish, will he give him a serpent? If ye then, being evil, know how to give good gifts unto your children, how much more shall your Father which is in heaven give good things to them that ask him?" Jesus, pointing to the sacred relationship of a father to his son, said in effect: "Multiply that by infinity and you will know what God is like."

There are many people who believe, in a general way, that God is their heavenly Father. They cannot, however, think of him as the Guardian of each individual life. They will point you at once to the mass of men and women in the world, with their incredible blindness and follies; their stupidities, jealousies, and hates. "It is impossible to believe," they say, "that God can love people like that or be their heavenly Father." But what is it that prompts us so to judge our fellow creatures? Is it not our own pride, narrowness, and prejudice? We are ascribing to God the limitations of our own love and sympathy. How often we have reason to be ashamed of the judgments that we pass upon people!

There comes to my mind this morning the recollection of an incident that happened in the Twenty-first Casualty Clearing Station at Merville, France, during the Great War. In the cot next to mine lay an English soldier, uneducated, rough, and rather repulsive looking. His head was swathed in bandages. Instinctively I experienced a feeling of dislike for this man and discouraged his friendly overtures. But one day, after we had conversed for a little while, he told me about his home, his wife, and his little girl Jennie, eight years of age. Then he took from the breast pocket of his tunic, which hung on a chair, a soiled and crumpled letter and passed it to me. This is the message that was written on it in the large, round letters of a child's hand:

Dear Daddy:

I think of you often. Each night I pray to Jesus to keep you safe and bring you back to your little girl.

With love,
Jennie.

As I passed back the letter to him I saw that his eyes were flooded with tears. "Isn't that a great letter?" he asked with fatherly pride. A feeling of shame swept over me for my superficial judgment of a fellow soldier. He was just another member of the Father's great family.

If we could but realize that each of us has an individual claim upon God, then we should be more considerate of others, remembering that they, too, are his children. We should also be more courageous. This belief was the rock upon which Jesus' faith was founded. When the enemies of the Master had completed all their plans for his death on the Cross, he, aware of what lay ahead of him, was undismayed. To his disciples he said: "Ye shall be scattered every man to his own and shall leave me alone: and yet I am not alone because the Father is with me."

Garrisoned by such a faith we shall triumph in life's darkest hour: temptations may come, misfortunes may come, sorrows may come, illness and death may come; but they will not find us unprepared, for we shall have a confidence that nothing can overthrow.

The death of Mr. G. K. Chesterton, the news of which has come to New York this morning, brings to mind one of his whimsical yet searching paragraphs. The question which he would ask a prospective landlady was not, "What is your charge for lodgings?" but rather, "What is your view of the universe?"

Like F. W. H. Myers, Chesterton realized that the issue of every crisis in life will be determined by our view of the universe. If we believe with the skeptic that the universe has "no purpose, heart, or mind or will," then indeed our case is desperate. But no follower of Christ is driven to this extremity. For the Christian, this is the Father's world, created by his wisdom and sustained by his power, with man as its goal and crown.

Let us then give ourselves with unceasing devotion to the task of building a world society that will be a fit dwelling place for God's children.

Then when our little day is drawing to a close; when the shadows are lengthening from the west and the earth and earthly things are drifting forever from our sight, death for us will be not a plunge into the dark profound of a hostile universe, but a falling asleep, like a tired child, in our Father's arms.

HAS RUSSIA BANISHED GOD?

And arms shall stand on his part, and they shall pollute the sanctuary of strength, and shall take away the daily sacrifice, and they shall place the abomination that maketh desolate.

DANIEL 11:31

HISTORY has witnessed many attempts to abolish religion and banish God. My text for this morning refers to one of these.

Antiochus Epiphanes, who became King of Syria in the year 175 B.C., undertook the subjugation of Palestine. It was his policy to conquer and Hellenize as much of the world as possible.

The Greek king made a surprise attack upon Jerusalem and captured the city. After having massacred many of its inhabitants, he established his military forces within the temple area and declared that Jewish religious observances were illegal. All sacrifice was abolished. The sacred books were destroyed; and even Sabbath observance was prohibited.

But the crowning indignity of all was committed by Antiochus, when, in December 168 B.C., he set up an altar to a pagan deity in the heart of the temple and then, to complete the desecration in the eyes of the Jews, he sacrificed swine upon that altar. This was the abomination that maketh desolate. So great was the indignation of the Hebrew people that the Maccabees, the father and his five sons, led a spontaneous uprising against the king, who, when he saw his purposes frustrated, went mad, and died shortly afterwards.

Little did that despotic monarch realize that not only would his attempts to blot out the Hebrew Faith meet with complete frustration, but that from out of that race, which he despised and persecuted, would come forth One who would establish a religion destined to achieve universal supremacy.

We move forward to the eighteenth century of the Christian era. There we find another attempt to abolish religion and banish God. In the year 1789 came the French Revolution. In its initial stages it was bloodless and held high promise for the future; but the reins of power passed into the hands of extremists, and there followed the unspeakable Terror. The king, queen, other members of the royal family, nobility, and leading citizens in all walks of life joined the long procession that was constantly moving from the prisons to the guillotine. The slaughter reached its peak when Robespierre came into power. In five weeks he sent twelve hundred and eighty-five people to their death, at the rate of seventy or eighty a day, until a special sewer had to be built in what is now the Place de la Concorde in Paris to carry away the crimson tide that flowed from the place of execution.

The leaders of the Revolution proclaimed that France had done with religion. It was to be forthwith abolished and God was to be banished from the land of "liberty, equality, fraternity." To make their declaration more impressive a parade was organized through the streets of Paris to Notre Dame Cathedral.

With graphic phrases Thomas Carlyle, in his *History of the French Revolution,* describes the scene. The new religion is to be the religion of Reason. Atheism must now become supreme. A goddess must, of course, be found to symbolize the worship of Reason and so, says Carlyle, Demoiselle Candeille of the Opera, "a woman fair to look upon, when well rouged," was selected. She was borne shoulder high at the head of the procession, "with red woollen nightcap; in azure mantle; garlanded with oak; holding in her hand the Pike of the Jupiter-*Peuple*: heralded by white young women girt in tricolor." This Opera singer, escorted by wild music, was placed upon the high altar of Notre Dame, while, in the midst of the cathedral, the frantic mob danced the fierce carmagnole until they fell in delirium and exhaustion.

While this was going on within the cathedral some of the celebrants climbed to the roof of Notre Dame and tore down the cross from the steeple, hurling it to the streets below where it was splintered into a thousand fragments.

It was proclaimed that God had been driven out and religion forever abolished. "The abomination that maketh desolate" once again appeared in the midst of the sanctuary where the multitudes had been wont to worship God. But how futile has been the attempt is witnessed today by the millions of both Protestants and Catholics who worship God in the land where it was purposed that atheism should reign supreme.

The third attempt to banish God has come in our own day. Most of you will recall the interest and the apprehension with which the whole world learned that Russia was in a state of revolution in 1917. It is not my purpose now to deal with the political and economic aspects of the Bolshevik revolt, important as these are. At a later date I hope, on the lecture platform, to speak of these matters. Today we are concerned with the religious aspects of the Revolution.

It is interesting to note that, in 1917, the Revolution in Russia was initiated by the moderates and, like the early stages of the French Revolution, gave promise of a new breath of freedom for the land in which it had taken place. That this hope has been disappointed is due to the fact that the Revolution passed, like the one in France, into the hands of extremists.

The procession of Russian citizens who were led to their doom by the Bolsheviks was ten times greater than the victims of the guillotine in France. They are numbered by hundreds of thousands and include people from every walk of life. For a decade and a half Russia has suffered from the loss of the best brains of the nation—a loss that cannot be made good for generations.

Like the revolutionaries in France, the Russian extremists sent the royal family to their doom. One of the horrible tragedies of history was enacted in a dark cellar under a dwelling house in a Siberian town, when a band of Bolshevik executioners shot down, in cold blood, the royal party of eleven, sparing not even the women and the children. When the news of this massacre leaked out of Russia, in spite of all attempts to suppress it, a shudder of revulsion swept over the whole world.

It was quite apparent from the first that the leaders of the Revolution were intensely hostile to religion. Their attitude is partly explained, when we remember that the established Church of Russia was little more than a department of State, with the Czar at its head. It is quite true that the priests of the Orthodox Church for centuries taught the people the duty of subjection to the Czar and to his authority. When the Revolution took place this body at once took sides against it and, on January 19, 1918, within two months of the coming into power of Lenin, the Patriarchate of Russia threw down the gantlet to the leaders of the Revolution, vehemently denouncing it and appealing to the people to rally against "these monsters of the human race."

Four days later came the Bolshevik reply. All control over education was taken away from the Church. All its property passed into the hands of the State and definite restrictions were placed upon religious leaders. In the years that followed much harsher edicts have been enacted.

Priests and ministers of religion are heavily taxed. They must pay exorbitant rent for their lodgings. They are forbidden the use of the mails, of telegraph and telephone communication. They cannot send or receive money orders, parcels, or letters.

When in Russia on a recent visit, I had interviews at different times with individual priests of the Orthodox Church. They talked freely of the serious handicaps under which they labored. In some sections, they told us, the priests had difficulty in obtaining food sufficient to keep them alive and well. They freely admitted the faults that had existed in the Orthodox Church before the Revolution, but they declared that the persecution which that Church has suffered in the past fifteen years has purified it of age-old evils and that a new spirit of heroism is evident today among the religious leaders akin to that which existed in the early days of Christianity, when the bloodthirsty Emperor Nero was ferreting out the followers of Christ in the homes and streets of pagan Rome.

The Soviet Government declares, of course, that it grants freedom of religion to all its citizens who desire to worship. That is true so long as the services of the Orthodox Church are restricted to masses and prayers. No one is allowed to interfere with these. On several occasions I visited Orthodox Cathedrals. In one case, on a Saturday night, between twelve hundred and thirteen hundred people were at the service. A fair proportion of young people was present. A few workmen there were dressed as though they had just come from their labors. It was a memorable experience for me. Seldom have I listened to such glorious singing. The main choir was made up of about thirty voices with an antiphonal choir of fifteen. All the choir members were comparatively young. The large congregation entered with deep sincerity into the service and the music was unforgettable.

While this measure of freedom is given to the Churches, the Christian people in Russia know well that the Government is set upon the extermination of their beloved Faith.

The Soviet Government's claim that it allows freedom of religion in Russia appears, superficially, to be true and has sometimes deceived visitors to that country. When we investigate the matter closely, however, we discover that the hands of religious leaders are tied by the fact that no religious instruction or propaganda among the people is permitted. Practically every theological school in the country has been closed, thus cutting off the source of supply of priests and ministers.

While religious instruction is illegal, antireligious propaganda is made legal and deliberately encouraged by the Government which claims that it is giving a fair chance to religion. Under Government auspices, in every city and town of Russia, there are antireligious museums generally set up in cathedrals and chapels that have been taken from the Orthodox Church. All manner of blasphemous and antireligious cartoons and symbols are exhibited in these places.

As we motored through the country districts of Russia, I observed every now and again a church from which the cross had been removed. Generally, in these churches, one finds on the altar a picture or bust of Lenin.

So, once again in history, we see "the abomination that maketh desolate" set up in the sanctuary.

The most effective effort toward making Russia a nation of atheists is carried out in the universities and schools. Atheism is taught in every kindergarten, school, and college in Russia. It is taught under the direction of the Government. There are many antireligious colleges in the Soviet Union. These are mainly night schools for the discussion of ways and means for suppressing religion. They train organizers and speakers. They educate writers of antireligious propaganda and produce curators for antireligious museums. Large universities have special faculties for training in atheism. Many theological libraries in the nation have been scrapped or else changed into atheistic libraries.

At a meeting of the Seventeenth All-Russian Party Congress, the President of the League of Militant Atheism declared: "Give us five more years and we will wipe out the last vestiges of religion in Russia. By 1937 we can accomplish the liquidation of God."

In a country district, about five hundred miles south of Moscow, we visited a school. After the children had been dismissed, I talked with a boy sixteen years of age. He was a bright, intelligent-looking lad. A member of our party said to him, "Do you believe in having icons in your home?" "No," said the boy, "I certainly do not." "Why?" we asked him. "Because," he said, "you use those things when you believe in God and I don't believe in God." "Why don't you believe in God?" The boy laughed and said, "Because there is no God." "How do you know that there is no God?" we asked him. "I know," he said, "because I have been taught that in school by our teacher, and I have read it in schoolbooks. I would throw the icons out the window," he declared, laughing heartily at the idea of the existence of God.

By its policy of teaching atheism to the children from the time they enter kindergarten at the age of three, and at the same time prohibiting all religious teaching, the Government has been successful in sowing the seeds of disbelief in the minds of millions of the young. Undoubtedly the next generation will witness in Russia a very great advance in the growth of atheism, and thousands of Orthodox churches and cathedrals which are now functioning will then be vacant and dismantled.

An official of the Orthodox Church, who occupies a high position in that body in Russia today and whose name and title must not be revealed, told us that there are at least seven thousand churches still open in Russia in spite of the fact that many thousands have been closed or torn down. There are still millions of people, he said, who attend church services, disregarding the persecution to which they are subjected. In many cases church attendance on the part of a worker will prove to be a serious obstacle in the way of promotion in his employment. It prohibits his playing any part in the government of the country, because a member of the Communist Party must, first of all, be an avowed and militant atheist. Yet, with amazing persistency, the people cleave to their Faith which is dearer to them today than ever before.

What is the meaning of all this for us in the United States? We are bound to feel the influence of this aggressive antireligious movement. Already, in this nation, there are many organizations working for the overthrow of our Faith. The Union of Militant Atheists of Russia is a member of an international organization of atheists called "The International of the Proletarian Free Thinkers." The Russian body is helping this organization, with which it is affiliated, to carry on its atheistic propaganda in various countries of the world including the United States.

I have been led to preach this sermon because in our nation there is a group of people among its ministers and its religious educators who believe that Communists are not seriously bent upon the extermination of religion; that Christian churches and organizations ought freely to cooperate with them and thereby win their good will; that if the Christian Church and its ministers and educators would but use some of the slogans of Communism, and make common cause with the believers in the Russian ideal, then they should find that the Communists, after all, are the real friends of religion.

Quite recently I have read articles printed in responsible Christian journals, in which certain religious leaders who have visited Russia are now declaring that the reasons why the Soviet Government is opposed to the Orthodox Church in Russia are that its teaching was based on superstition, that it was allied with the Czarist Government, and that it assisted in the exploitation of the masses. It would have been entirely different, they are suggesting, if religion in Russia had been like that which they propose—philosophical, humanistic, and essentially social in its emphasis. Therefore, what the Church in this country ought to do now, they say, is to cooperate with the Communists against war, Fascism, and other evils that are abroad in the world. Not for one moment would I suggest that these writers are dishonest, but I am positively convinced that they are entirely mistaken in their judgment of Communism, whether in Russia or in this nation.

While in the Soviet Union I talked with representatives of the Government, with newspapermen, and with well-known writers of whom Karl Radek was one. The unanimous declaration of all these citizens of Russia was that Communism stands unalterably opposed to religion in every form and that Communists will never rest until every vestige of religion is eliminated from the countries in which they live.

I hold in my hand the Program of the Communist International which I purchased in Moscow. In it are given instructions to Communists, in all countries of the world, on the conduct of propaganda. This program declares emphatically that "one of the most important tasks of the cultural revolution affecting the great masses is the task of systematically and unswervingly combating religion, the opium of the people." This can best be accomplished, it asserts, by antireligious propaganda and by atheistic instruction in the schools.

I could cite many Russian authorities who flatly contradict the assertion that it is only a special brand of religion that the Communists oppose. Time will permit me to quote from only one. Few men understand the religious situation in Russia more clearly than does Professor Julius F. Hecker, who was born and educated in that country and who came to the United States and received the degree of Doctor of Philosophy here. He was at one time a teacher in a theological school in Russia. For some years he was under the suspicion of the Soviet but is now a professor in one of its universities. In his book *Religion and Communism* Professor Hecker says:

> There is a tendency among some writers on Communism to ignore the religious issue, or to regard it as a misunderstanding, interpreting Communists' opposition to organized religion as an opposition to the abuses of

religion, but not to religion in its pure state. This is a great error. Communists, particularly Lenin, have always emphasized that reformed, modernized, socialized, and every other improved religion is worse than the old Orthodox reactionary religion. As a matter of fact, Communists are much more tolerant to reactionary religion than to any of its modernized and philosophically improved forms.

That statement is a clear and true presentation of the facts of the case and religious leaders who seek to make a common front with Communists, in the hope that their good will may thereby be secured for religion, are deceiving nobody but themselves.

While it is true that "the abomination of desolation" is triumphant in many parts of Russia today, we may well ask the questions: What about the distant future? Will the Soviet Government yet succeed in banishing God? The only person who can believe that is the one who labors under the curious delusion that the existence of God depends upon the good will of the Government that happens to be in power. Make no mistake about it, God is still on the throne. Millions of Russians continue to worship him. I have not the slightest fear of the ultimate fate of religion in Russia. Few people in the world are so spiritual. Their profoundly mystical temperament impels them to cleave naturally to faith.

That Soviet leaders themselves are afraid of what may happen is clearly evidenced by the fact that they have silenced, exiled, or slain practically all the evangelical preachers in Russia. A friend of mine who is a Baptist minister in Toledo, Ohio, attended the

1934 World Conference of Baptists in Germany. He asked one of the officials to give him the names of some of the Baptist preachers in Russia. This man replied that the most careful investigation revealed only one Baptist minister remaining there; the rest had been exiled, imprisoned, or shot. He declared that, under no circumstances, would he reveal the name and address of this minister because such an act would probably bring about this man's death.

Why is the Government afraid of these evangelical ministers? Obviously it fears them much more than it does the Orthodox Church. The reason is this: no sooner had the Communist Government of Russia granted freedom to them than they went throughout the nation preaching the Gospel of Christ. The Soviet leaders were startled to discover that whole towns and districts which had previously been won over by atheistic propaganda were now swept anew by a religious movement of throbbing spiritual life. More than a million converts were made in a period of about two years. As a result, one by one, these prophetic voices in Russia have been silenced. In many cases, in the darkness of the night, a knock sounded on a minister's door; then followed a swift trial before the tribunal of the secret police, and he disappeared from sight.

What will be the issue of all this? We have reason to rejoice in the increasing literacy of the masses in Russia and in the slowly rising standard of living, notably among city people. History has demonstrated that you cannot keep a nation permanently enslaved, especially as it grows in intelligence. The number of radio aerials that can be seen on the roof of apartments also gives promise for the future. The day is coming when a door of opportunity will open for religion in Russia, not because the leaders of the Government will have relented, but because the nation will have demanded it. They will want to know something about the faith of people in other lands. When that hour strikes, a new field of missionary opportunity will be open to the Christian world. By radio, through the press, and by the spoken word, the Gospel will be preached to Russia.

Having met and talked with its people, who are kind hearted and hospitable, and particularly with its highly idealistic youth, I have not the slightest misgivings as to the outcome. No nation can continue to exist on a philosophy of negation. The day will come when the people of Russia will learn that man cannot live by bread alone. Even when all their material needs have been satisfied, they will yet have problems, ethical, social, and moral, that religion alone can solve.

If it were possible to separate the social and economic program of the Communist from his anti-religious campaign, then there might be some reason for cooperation between Christian churches and Communists. But this separation Communists have steadfastly refused to make. They are determined to seek the overthrow of all religion and the establishment in its stead of universal atheism. An important document issued by the governing body of Soviet Russia declares:

"It is necessary to condemn categorically, as the worst type of popery, every approachment of Christianity to Communism. Religion must be rejected for good, without reservation and camouflage."

In spite of the hostility revealed in such declarations as this the Christian Church must not adopt an attitude of condescension toward Communists. While energetically combating their attempt to replace our democratic institutions with a Communist dictatorship and to turn the churches and chapels of this nation into antireligious museums, we must dedicate ourselves as never before to the elimination of economic ills such as unemployment and social injustice which are constant breeders of disaffection and unrest. The best antidote to Communism is genuine Christianity expressing itself in every segment of our national life. If we are true to the high ideals of the Kingdom of God we may face the future unafraid.

No matter how startling may be the developments that humanity will make through the powerful aid of an unsleeping science; no matter how vast may be the achievements of the intellect of man, as he continues to delve into the mysteries of the universe; no matter how intensive may be the propaganda of atheism throughout the world, this, at least, is sure—religion will abide in unshaken power, because God has planted its roots deep within the human soul and because he is undefeatable in his purposes for his children.

A GIFT OF GOD—A GOOD MOTHER

Moreover his mother made him a little coat, and brought it to him from year to year, when she came up with her husband to offer the yearly sacrifice.

I SAMUEL 2:19

IN THE year 1823 a new opera was performed at the Covent Garden theater, London. It was entitled *The Maid of Milan.* I am sure that its composer would have been greatly surprised had he learned that it was destined to make him immortal. His fame is due, however, not to the opera as a whole, but merely to one song that occurs in it. This little poem is known and loved the world over. The night on which it was first sung in that London theater it touched a chord that vibrated in millions of human hearts. The title of this song, written by John Howard Payne, American author and playwright, is "Home, Sweet Home."

What beautiful and fragrant memories cluster round that word "home"! Who can analyze its content or fathom its meaning? Immediately we think of another word equally dear to our hearts, "Mother." "Home and Mother!" These words belong to each other. They are inseparable. So precious are they that we carry over into our religious faith the associations which they convey. We speak of Heaven as "Home"—the Home of the soul. When God sought to convey to the children of Israel a realization of his loving care, he said, "As one whom his mother comforteth, so will I comfort you."

Twenty-eight years ago the first "Mother's Day" service was held in a little Virginia town. It originated in a memorial service in honor of a mother who had spent her strength in the service of Christ. Six years later, in 1914, the second Sunday in May was set apart officially as "Mother's Day" by resolution of Congress and by proclamation of the President of the United States. In the last few years a definite reaction against the celebration of Mother's Day has appeared in some quarters. It has sprung up because of the orgy of emotionalism that has characterized some of the services honoring motherhood. Also, the day has been so commercialized that some people have even suggested that it should no longer be observed in Christian churches. But if these be valid reasons for abandoning the celebration we might as well abolish Christmas too, for the objections urged against the one day apply with equal force to the other. Such an extreme course will be advocated only by people who cannot distinguish between sentiment, which rules our lives in many particulars, and sentimentalism. For some of us Mother's Day has brought gains that are too precious to be lightly cast away.

One of the most practical ways in which to commemorate this day would be for each of us to take an intelligent interest in the provisions recently made for dependent mothers. We should regard it as an obligation of honor to insure that the sunset years of mothers whose children have been unable to care for them are not filled with hardship and sadness. On this day we ought also to recall the part that religion inevitably plays in the life of every true mother.

In the ancient story, from which our text is taken, we are introduced to a Hebrew mother whose name was Hannah. Like so many Hebrew names it has a beautiful connotation. It signifies "Grace." Hannah was the wife of Elkanah of Mount Ephraim. For years she sorrowed over the fact that she had no child. In ancient Israel it was believed that the childless wife was under the curse of God. Hannah was bowed down with grief because of this affliction.

Then came the time for the annual feast, in the Temple of Jehovah, at Shiloh. The wife of Elkanah, kneeling in the sanctuary, prayed that God, in his mercy, give to her a child. She requested that it might be a boy and pledged herself to dedicate him, from his birth, to the Divine service. As Hannah continued praying she felt in her soul the inflowing peace of God, which comes from conscious communion with him; and when she left the Temple to travel back to her distant home she journeyed with a light heart. She believed that God would answer her petition. The Scripture says: "Her countenance was no more sad." Her soul had found rest at last, for she had tasted of the experience of which the Prophet speaks: "Thou wilt keep him in perfect peace whose mind is stayed on thee, because he trusteth in thee." The mother's faith was rewarded. Her prayer was answered. A baby boy was born to her and she called his name Samuel.

The mother's gratitude to God is revealed in the fact that the name "Samuel" means "Asked of the Lord" or "Heard of the Lord." She wished the name of her son to be a perpetual memorial to the fact that God answers prayer.

This Hebrew mother, having received her heart's desire, did not forget the vow that she had made. As soon as her child was old enough to be separated from his parents, she took him to the Temple at Shiloh and dedicated him to God. To Eli, the High Priest, she said: "For this child I prayed; and the Lord hath given me my petition which I asked of him: Therefore also I have lent him to the Lord; as long as he liveth he shall be lent to the Lord."

Even the name of Hannah's child is a rebuke to those parents who, in our own day, never think of God in connection with their children; who have never thanked him for the precious gift of little ones who have come to make our homes resound with happy laughter.

We seldom realize what a solemnizing responsibility is ours in the heritage of children. We have received from the hand of God little ones whose lives may be a blessing to the world, or whose memory men may curse for the sorrows that they cause. The almost creative influence of parents over children will determine most often what the child will become. Remember that your children are God's gift to you—a sacred trust. That fact is recognized in the Sacrament of Baptism. We take our little ones to God's House and, like Hannah of old, we dedicate them to him; and pledge ourselves, in his presence, to bring them up in the nurture and admonition of the Lord.

It was no small sacrifice for Hannah and her husband to leave this lad in the Temple; but the mother faithfully observed the vow that she had made to God before Samuel was born.

The High Priest, Eli, who ministered in the Temple at Shiloh had become an old man. He was sad and lonely because his own sons had disgraced him. His eyesight had become dim, and his step was growing feeble. He needed just such a lad as Samuel to help him in the Temple.

Samuel was very proud of the linen ephod which he wore to mark him out as an assistant of the High Priest. "He was the door-keeper of God's House at Shiloh. He opened the doors of the Tabernacle in the morning and shut them again at night. At sunset he would carefully trim and light the candles in the seven-branch candlestick, and at sunrise he would extinguish them again. He ran messages for Eli. He did everything that quick little hands and quick little feet could do to keep the House of God in order and beauty."

Samuel had his hours of homesickness when he thought of his mother far away, but the bright spot in his life was the knowledge that at least once a year she and his father would come to visit him at Shiloh. As the time drew near he would say to Eli, "In seven days Mother will be here again"; and later, "Isn't it wonderful? Tomorrow Mother will come!"

We may be sure, too, that Hannah in far-off Ramah did not close her eyes in sleep, even one night, without asking God to bless her little boy in the Temple at Shiloh. Throughout all the year her mind would be upon their next meeting. Not only did she think about her boy, but she was constantly planning and working for him too. Our text says, "His mother made him a little coat, and brought it to him from year to year, when she came up with her husband to offer the yearly sacrifice."

In the Old Testament you will notice frequent references to the loom. You read of the pin, the shuttle, and the thrum. Many Hebrew women wove, on the loom, all the clothing that was worn by their families. Weaving had become a high art in Egypt long before the Israelites had left on their exodus. Undoubtedly, the Jews had learned the art in that land.

I am sure that Hannah's love went into every stitch that she put on the garment. How carefully she would choose the wool with which to weave the cloth! Then it would have to be dyed so that the bright colors would gladden little Samuel's heart. Many days would be spent at the loom. Every now and then she would turn to Elkanah and say, "Father, do you think that this coat is going to be big enough for Samuel? Last year it was a little too small." So her busy fingers worked until the coat was ready for her boy. Little gifts such as would gladden a boy's heart were put into the parcel with the new coat.

In France during the Great War many a soldier lad marveled at the thoughtfulness of a mother. When the mail had come and the parcels were opened, little gifts were found that only a mother would think of. She knew best the needs and desires of her boy.

The miles must have seemed long to Hannah as she journeyed from Ramah to Shiloh! No sooner had the parents come in sight of the Temple than little Samuel would rush out eagerly and fling himself into his parents' arms. Hannah would take out the little coat, a bit larger than the one she had made in the previous year, and try it on her boy. Then she would turn to her husband with a look of dismay and say, "Didn't I tell you? Look, Father, the sleeves are too short. I will have to let them out. My, how that boy does grow!"

Every hour they were together on these yearly visits the Hebrew mother gave to her lad wise counsel and motherly advice.

Then came a day when Samuel waited in vain for the yearly visit. Not again would his mother come bearing her gifts and the new coat; for a few months before, God had called her to a better Home than the little cottage in Ramah.

The little boy Samuel grew into a young man full of promise, who wore a prophet's mantle. All Israel knew of Samuel's mantle. Apparently it was a distinguishing mark. I think he must always have worn the same colors that his mother had put into the little coat. The name of the prophet was known all over the land, and many people came to visit him. When his dearest friends arrived he would produce a little coat, carefully folded away, and would say, "This is the last coat that Mother ever made for me, and she made it with her own hands."

The first lesson we learn from this old, old story is the faithfulness of a mother's love.

Hannah never disappointed her boy. Each year the

coat was ready, and the long journey to Shiloh was as nothing because at its close she would see her son. Isn't that true of all good mothers? They live for their children. They plan, they toil, they sacrifice for them; and they count it all a joy.

May I remind you boys and girls here this morning of the fact that oftentimes you accept quite thoughtlessly the service of your mother? No matter how tired she is, there is always time to sew on a few more buttons, to lace up little shoes, or to put some stitches into a baseball glove. And sometimes little people forget to say "Thank you."

None of us could ever repay the debt we owe to our mothers. Have you forgotten the days and nights when you were sick with measles or scarlet fever or diphtheria? Do you remember how you tossed restlessly on the pillow, when out of the dark there came those weird and terrible images hovering around you, phantoms that fever had conjured up? You called out to Mother. Immediately her presence chased all the shadows away. Her hand felt cool upon your heated brow. "It was she who held the cup of cold water to your lips; who bent over you day and night, and fought away with almost supernatural strength the greatest of all enemies—Death."

Even though everyone else should cease to believe in us, her faith would remain unshaken to the end. There is nothing in all the wide, wide world so wonderful as the faithfulness of a mother's love.

Finally, we learn from this incident how the world is made better by the influence of a good mother.

Who can estimate all that was accomplished by the life of the prophet Samuel? We must never forget, however, that his achievements were made possible by the influence of a mother who dedicated her boy to God.

If we could have asked Samuel what he considered to be the greatest factor in the formation of his character, I am sure that he would have answered, "My mother's faith and my mother's prayers."

I am thinking this morning of a twentieth-century mother whose name was Hannah. She, too, had a boy who became a prophet of God. He never wearied of acknowledging his indebtedness to her. "At my mother's knee," he once said, "I gained my sweetest inspirations." The name of this man was John Henry Jowett.

Samuel was a judge in Israel as well as a prophet. He was called upon to adjudicate all important cases in the nation. When he was come near to the end of his long pilgrimage, in the presence of many thousands of the people of Israel he said: "I am old and grayheaded; and . . . I have walked before you from my childhood unto this day. Behold, here I am: witness against me before the Lord. . . . Whom have I defrauded? Whom have I oppressed? or of whose hand have I received any bribe to blind mine eyes therewith? and I will restore it you." All the multitude answered: "Thou hast not defrauded us, nor oppressed us, neither hast thou taken ought of any man's hand." What a tribute was that paid, by a whole people, to one who had lived his life in their midst!

Israel was ennobled by the influence of the prophet Samuel. Who can estimate the value, to a nation, of one great man? What did David Livingstone and

William Ewart Gladstone mean to Great Britain? What have Dwight L. Moody, Thomas A. Edison, and Abraham Lincoln meant to America? Yet all of these whom I have named declared that everything they achieved in life they owed to their mothers. John Randolph of Roanoke, the American orator and statesman, says, in a letter written to a friend, that it was the memory of his mother's prayers which saved him in the greatest crisis of his career.

> I reached the place in my life in which I was ready to cast aside Christianity and all faith in God [he said]. I was standing on the brink of an abyss. In that very hour there came back to me a memory. It was the memory of one night when the lamp was lighted on the table, and I was kneeling by my mother, and she took my little hands in hers and said, "I want you to say with me: Our Father which art in heaven." It was that recollection that saved me.

The most blessed influence in this world is the power of a mother's prayers. Hannah, praying in her little home at Ramah, is influencing the life of Samuel in far-off Shiloh. There are some of us who will carry to the last moment of life, as its sweetest recollection, the memory of a mother's prayers. May I say to the mothers here: There are many things that you can do for your children which will mean much in making them fine, wholesome, noble; but nothing else is half so important as the prayers that you offer for them at the Throne of Grace.

Margaret Widdemer, in her poem "The Watcher-Mother," has expressed feelingly the central theme of our text when she says:

She always leaned to watch for us,
  Anxious if we were late,
In winter by the window,
  In summer by the gate;

And though we mocked her tenderly,
  Who had such foolish care,
The long way home would seem more safe
  Because she waited there.

Her thoughts were all so full of us—
  She never could forget!
And so I think that where she is
  She must be watching yet.

Waiting till we come home to her,
  Anxious if we are late—
Watching from heaven's window,
  Leaning from heaven's gate.

OUR PROTESTANT HERITAGE

I. Is Protestantism "Bankrupt"?

Stand fast therefore in the liberty wherewith Christ hath made us free, and be not entangled again with the yoke of bondage.

GALATIANS 5:1

ANYONE who is guilty of feeding the fires of intolerance or of increasing the spirit of religious prejudice in our day has committed a crime against mankind. He has rendered a disservice to the Christian Church as well. It is the height of folly for one branch of the Church to attack another in a time when mighty forces are attempting the complete overthrow of all religion.

On the one hand Communism has set itself steadfastly to the extermination of religion, root and branch. Its advocates declare that nothing will turn them aside from their purpose of making atheism universal. On the other hand, Fascism seeks to throttle religion or to make it merely the mouthpiece of autocratic and materialistic leaders.

In such a threatening world situation it ill behooves believers in Christ to battle with one another when they have in common implacable foes who are seeking their downfall. That does not mean, however, that we are to surrender our individual convictions, that we need no longer maintain the Faith of our fathers. The Protestant pulpit in recent years has sadly neglected its teaching function. Many of our people, young and old, are pathetically ignorant of the fundamentals of our Faith. It is my purpose to emphasize afresh in this church a teaching as well as a preaching ministry. Intolerance flourishes best of all in an atmosphere of ignorance. If we are informed on the subject of our own Faith, we are much more likely to respect the convictions of others who differ from us. Whatever may be the weaknesses of the Roman Catholic Church this, at least, is sure: that Church has never failed to instruct her people. It is, therefore, an informed tolerance that I am striving for in this series of Sunday-morning sermons.

This subject has been thrust upon our attention by an appeal signed by a group of twenty-nine High Churchmen of the Protestant Episcopal Communion. The document was addressed to the bishops of that Church and to many of its ministers. It declared, among other things, that "Protestantism, once the religion of by far the greater part of the American people, is bankrupt ethically, culturally, morally and religiously. Its driving force, negative at best, has exhausted itself and it has ceased to attract or to inspire." The severest condemnation of this intemperate document has come from the leadership of the Episcopal Church itself.

We have here a striking illustration of the absurd lengths to which even educated people will go when their zeal outruns their judgment. The assertion which they make regarding Protestantism in this nation is, of course, unkind, unjust, and untrue. Protestantism, far from being bankrupt, is at this hour a spiritual dynamic in the lives of millions of American Christians. I can conceive of no greater tragedy overtaking this nation than that the enlightening and ennobling influence which Protestantism exerts today upon every segment of the life of the American people should suddenly be removed.

Moreover when the High Churchmen who drew up this amazing document referred to the movement for reunion with Rome, which they have espoused, they were deceiving nobody but themselves. It is not reunion with Rome which they are advocating, but it is rather submission to the ecclesiastical authority of the Pope. Like Henry IV of Germany, who presented himself as a penitent on three successive days, standing barefoot in the snow outside the castle of Canossa, making humble submission to Pope Hildebrand, these clergymen of the Episcopal Church would forswear their allegiance to that honored branch of Christendom and abjectly surrender to the government of the Roman Pontiff.

Years ago the Roman Church rejected the claims of the Anglican Church, and as things stand today the only "reunion" that Rome will countenance is that of complete and unqualified submission.

In striking contrast to the misguided efforts of the Episcopal clergymen to whom I have referred is the attitude of Bishop Manning of New York. In his recent essay on the subject, "The Sin of Disunion," he is not misled by empty talk about reunion. He declares that the Episcopal Church can render its greatest contribution to the cause of a united Christendom by maintaining its position as a *via media* or middle way between Roman Catholicism and Protestantism. He points out the folly of any church assuming for itself a place of supremacy; of one branch of Christendom looking at other branches with benevolent condescension and speaking of "our separated brethren," "schismatics," "heretics"! Says Bishop Manning, "There is no communion on earth, Catholic or Protestant, which is not a sharer in the sin [of disunion]."

The Roman Catholic Moehler echoes the same thought when he says that Catholics and Protestants "must stretch a friendly hand one to the other. Both conscious of guilt must exclaim, 'We have all erred.' "

Up to the present, one branch of Christianity has declined to do this. When eighty-six divisions of the Christian Church came together in the city of Lausanne, Switzerland, for a conference on Faith and Order, the Church of Rome was the only major body not represented there. The Pope later explained his refusal to send a delegate on the ground that he was prepared to receive the submission of all other churches but not to confer with them. It is this submission which a few of the leaders in the Episcopal Church are now prepared to make

On Christmas Day, 1931, Pope Pius XI issued his encyclical *"Lux Veritatis"* ("The Light of Truth"). In this encyclical the present Pope set forth clearly his attitude on the question of reunion. He invited the Protestant and Eastern Orthodox Churches to make their submission to him on two grounds: first, the Immaculate Conception of the Virgin Mary and, secondly, the dogma of Papal Infallibility. The "Immaculate Conception" did not become a dogma in the Church of Rome until the year 1854; and Papal Infallibility not until the year 1869.

If Pius XI had suggested that a basis of union might be found, not in Mary the mother of Jesus, or in his own infallibility, but in Jesus Christ whom St. Paul declares to be the Chief Cornerstone of the Church, then indeed might some progress have been made; but Christ was relegated to a minor place in the encyclical. As Bishop Manning has said, "the nearer we get to Christ the closer we Christians get to one another." But not once has the New Testament basis of fellowship been suggested by the Pope as a grounds for the reunion of Christendom.

Our Lord himself once said: "By this shall all men know that ye are my disciples if ye have love one to another." How far short have we Christians fallen from the standards of Jesus! Christians of all denominations believe in one God, owe allegiance to one Savior, and journey to one Eternal Home. They may transact business one with another, enjoy a common social life, and eat together, but they are forbidden to worship with one another.

So far as the Roman hierarchy is concerned, Protestant peoples might as well devote their thought and attention not to a will-o'-the-wisp possibility of reunion with Rome, but to healing the divisions within Protestantism and to making the witness of our Protestant churches to Christ more effective in the life of this nation.

Let us look now for a moment at the charge which has been made that Protestantism is bankrupt. The implication, of course, is that the Church of Rome in America is flourishing. A fair test of the vitality of a religious body would seem to be the percentage of increase in its adherents. In the year 1926 the religious census of this nation was taken. Due to the initiative of Dr. George Linn Kieffer of New York, whose annual summary of church statistics is published in the *Christian Herald*, we can form a true estimate of the advance made by the various religious bodies in this country. In the eight-year period after the 1926 census the increase of membership in the Roman Catholic Church has been 1.21 per cent. During the same period more than half a dozen Protestant bodies had a much larger increase than the Roman Catholic. The Lutheran increase was 1.64 per cent; the Methodist 1.40 per cent; the Baptist 2.35 per cent; the Evangelical and Reformed 4.41 per cent —in contrast to 1.21 per cent of increase in the Roman Catholic Church.

The percentage of increase of the largest Protestant churches in this nation has been definitely higher than that of the Roman Catholic Church. It must be remembered, too, that the Church of Rome counts among its adherents very young children who have been confirmed, so that the percentage of the adult increase of Protestantism is considerably higher even than it appears to be.

It would be unwise to draw too sweeping conclusions from religious statistics. But one thing, at least, is clear: no Christian Church in this nation is running away with the country, and certainly there is little basis in these statistics for the belief that the

Church of Rome is the only thriving religious organization in our midst.

One of the most frequent misconceptions entertained regarding Protestantism, as Dean Inge has pointed out, is that it represents a negative attitude to religion; that it lives by protesting against and attacking established forms of faith. This mistaken opinion is held by the Episcopal group which drafted the appeal that we have examined. They say, speaking of Protestantism, "Its driving force, negative at best, has exhausted itself."

One of the reasons for this notion is that the word "Protestant" is misunderstood. Most people think that it means merely an objector, one who is always opposing beliefs or policies. That idea, of course, is quite wrong. A protestant, as the use of the word in Reformation times reveals, means one who makes a protestation. Webster in his unabridged dictionary gives as the primary meaning of protestation, "a solemn declaration of fact, opinion or resolution." This is the meaning of the word in the time of Shakespeare and after. In *The Merchant of Venice* Gratiano says, "I have a wife whom I protest I love"; that is, "whom I declare or affirm that I love."

The negative meaning of a dissenter is much later than the original application of the name to the Reformers. When the Reichstag meeting in Speier, Germany, in 1529, voted to restrict the freedom of the Reformed Church, a solemn declaration was drawn up affirming the liberty of the Reformation Diets. This affirmation or protestation led to the Reformers being called Protestants.

In a very real sense Protestantism has its roots in

the Old Testament as well as in the New. The prophets of Israel were the Protestants of the Hebrew Faith. Frequently these prophets were compelled to point out the evils that had accompanied the ceremonials of the priests. In sacrifice and ritual, in precepts and prohibitions, they forget the weightier matters of the law—justice, mercy, and truth. The Prophet Micah makes this clear. He says to the people, "Wherewith shall I come before the Lord and bow myself before the High God? Shall I come before him with burnt offerings, with calves of a year old? Will the Lord be pleased with thousands of rams or with ten thousands of rivers of oil? . . . He hath showed thee, O man, what is good; and what doth the Lord require of thee, but to do justly and to love mercy and to walk humbly with thy God?"

That is exactly the spirit of the Protestant Reformation. Our Lord put himself in the Prophetic succession. He lived and died a Prophet. He was called "the Prophet of Nazareth." Some of the religious leaders feared and hated him because he disregarded the organization of priestly mediation in Jerusalem, revealing God as a Heavenly Father who could be sought and found by the humblest of his children, without the office of rabbi or priest; and proclaiming that the grace and forgiveness of God could be found by those who went into their own chamber and shut the door, communing with a Father who sees in secret and who rewards his children openly.

Jesus was the greatest emancipator in history. He lifted from men burdens grievous to be borne, that the priestly class had laid upon them. He was a Reformer in the highest sense of the term, because he made forever impossible the old Hebrew legalisms. Like a seed planted in a vessel Jesus buried his teaching in the Jewish Church. It grew into the mighty Tree of Christianity which burst through all restraining walls.

St. Paul, incomparably the greatest of the apostles, was the one who first discovered this fact. When some of his fellow apostles would have placed upon the Gentile Christians shackles and manacles belonging to old Jewish ceremonies like that of circumcision, St. Paul, the Protestant among the apostles, reminded them that Christ came to set men free, not to place them afresh in ecclesiastical bondage. His challenging words are found in our text: "Stand fast therefore in the liberty wherewith Christ hath made us free, and be not entangled again with the yoke of bondage."

What the Reformers accomplished in the sixteenth century was simply a repetition of the achievements of the Prophets of the Old Dispensation, of St. Paul, and of other forward-looking Christians in the New. They affirmed our liberty in Christ. The Reformers were distinguished not merely by active opposition to a corrupt church but rather by positive affirmations of Christian faith. They sought to regain the lost simplicities of religion as Jesus had taught it. They broke down the barriers of priestly mediation that had kept men and women from direct access to God.

The achievements of the Reformation may be summed up under four heads:

First, it laid the foundations of religious, intellectual, and civil liberty whereby every man has the inalienable right and privilege to seek for truth and to worship God as he chooses, none daring to make him afraid.

Second, it made possible the rise of modern democracy wherein the common people of every land, and not their rulers, shall have the final say in matters of government. In a day when dictatorships are flourishing once again and despotism sits enthroned in many a nation, the world needs as never before the witness of Protestantism with its unfailing demand for freedom.

Third, it put the Bible into the hands of the common people of Europe and cheered millions of lives by its radiant message of comfort and hope.

Fourth, it banished forever the notion that any church or hierarchy can, by the proclamation of an interdict, shut off a whole nation from God and the means of grace. Instead it has established the truth that the Bible teaches from Genesis to Revelation that God may be approached and salvation achieved without the intercession of priest or minister.

Eighteen months ago I stood in Oxford city, England, on the identical spot where the Protestant bishops, Latimer and Ridley, paid with their lives for their loyalty to the Reformation. As these devoted men stood in the public square, each chained to a stake, an executioner brought a lighted fagot and threw it down at Ridley's feet where the wood was piled about him. Bishop Latimer turned to his comrade in martyrdom and said, "Be of good cheer, Brother Ridley, and play the man. We shall this day light such a candle, by God's grace, in England as I trust shall never be put out." The light that was kindled that day in Oxford Town has grown from a candle flame to a mighty beacon of Truth, at which many a torch has been lighted down the centuries.

When we look back over the history of our Faith, what a thrill of pride sweeps over us as we think of all that Protestantism has meant to mankind; from what base fears it has freed us; what a glorious heritage it has bequeathed to us; what challenging prospects it holds out before us. But let us not forget that every privilege brings with it a corresponding responsibility. May we ever hold aloft the torch of Truth that has been flung to us until its kindling rays shall penetrate to earth's remotest bounds, carrying into lands where darkness and error reign the light and the love and the liberty of the Gospel of Jesus Christ.

OUR PROTESTANT HERITAGE

II. Can Protestantism Be United?

Is Christ divided?

I CORINTHIANS 1:13

ONE day about the year 55 A.D. a little group of men were seen walking along the highway toward the ancient city of Corinth. They had just come from Athens, the center of education and culture in Greece. They were approaching the capital city of the Roman Province where the seat of Government was located, and where industry and commerce held sway.

The city of Corinth bestrode the isthmus of that name, and had planted one foot in each of the seas that washed her shores. That is the reason why Horace in one of his odes speaks of "two-sea'd Corinth." Here was one of the most important cities of Greece. It lay on the highway between the East and West. Its harbors were always crowded with a forest of masts. In this cosmopolitan city material prosperity reigned. From the spacious harbors the land sloped up to the citadel which towered eighteen hundred feet above the city and was one of the most formidable of ancient fortresses.

Corinth was noted not only for its prosperity but also for its iniquity. The dominant religion in the city was the worship of the Goddess Aphrodite. This religion exerted a debasing influence on its adherents. Vice in its most unspeakable forms prevailed in this seaport city. So notorious was Corinth for viciousness that no greater insult could be offered to a citizen of Athens than to call him a Corinthian. The name was synonymous with debauchery.

In the center of the little group making its way into Corinth was a man of medium stature, with no physical beauty to commend him, but who by his every word and gesture revealed a dynamic personality. He carried under his arm a bundle in which were some needles and assorted threads, patches of canvas and a leather palm—the tools of the tentmaker's trade. Seeking out a family that followed his calling, he made his home with them. The man we have been observing was, of course, the Apostle Paul.

The ordinary run of men would have considered Corinth beyond redemption and a most unfruitful field for religious work; but the great Apostle, like his Master, had come to seek and to save that which was lost, and he regarded this wicked city as especially challenging. In it for fifteen months the Apostle preached the Gospel of Christ. When his little band of followers was no longer permitted to worship in the synagogue, it met week by week in a private home. In the midst of a pagan civilization, with ignorance, superstition, and immorality surrounding him on every side, St. Paul established a Christian Church. Even as a lighthouse sends its cheering rays across the dark waters to gladden the mariner's eye, so in this ancient city the church founded by St. Paul shed abroad into the surrounding darkness the light and the healing of the Gospel of Christ. St. Paul loved this church. In a very real sense it was his child. Its membership had been built up through his labors and his prayers. "You may have ten thousand instructors in Christ," Paul tells them, "but only one father." He calls them "Beloved children of mine."

After having established in the Faith this band of Christians, which was daily increasing in number, St. Paul set out to preach in other cities also; but he kept in constant contact with the Corinthian Church. After many months had passed he received a letter from the house of Chloe. The news which it contained greatly distressed the Apostle. He was informed that some time after he had left the little Christian community in Corinth a spirit of dissension had sprung up in it. A number of parties were formed. One group called itself by the name of Paul —the Pauline Party. "We," they said, "rally around the founder of this Church, the man who established it. We give our allegiance to him." Another group said, "We are the Apollos Party. We are the cultured people. We give our allegiance to the orator and scholar Apollos." Says Renan: "The talent of Apollos turned all their heads." How strange that the man who had been sent by Paul himself to Corinth should have become one of the factors in the divisions there!

But still another group declared, "We are the Cephas Party. We follow Simon Peter. He saw the Lord in the flesh. He was commissioned of Christ to be an Apostle. He was one of the original Twelve—

not like this upstart Paul, who has no valid commission to be an Apostle."

And finally there was the Christ Party. These claimed a monopoly of the Spirit of Christ. "You people," they said, "with all your divisions and your party cries have no valid claim upon the Church of Christ. We are the people who belong to him."

How Paul must have grieved to hear the news of these divisions! From a heart rent with anxiety he cries, "Is Christ divided?" Can you take Christ and parcel him out a little bit to this party and a little bit to that party? Can you divide the Body of our Lord which is his Church?

Anyone who reads with discernment Paul's Letter to the Corinthians can see in that little Christian community the embryo of modern divisions in the Christian Church. You can find for each of the parties that existed in Corinth a present-day parallel. There is the Peter Party which claims that it alone stands in the true succession of the Apostles. There is the Christ Party which claims that it has a monopoly of the grace and power of our Lord. And so on the parallel runs.

We who belong to that great body of Christian believers known as Protestants have every reason to glory in the achievements made possible centuries ago in the Reformation. We cannot, however, pride ourselves in the fact that Protestantism has sometimes carried to extremes its doctrine of liberty. The *reductio ad absurdum* of denominationalism can be seen by a study of the American religious census. There are some two hundred separate Christian bodies in this country. They are divided as follows:

18 branches of Baptists
17 Lutheran Churches
19 Methodist
9 Eastern Catholic and 3 Western Catholic including the Roman
16 Mennonite bodies
*9 separate Presbyterian divisions

and many others.

Not only are there a large number of separate denominations but these are themselves divided and subdivided.

Let us take one denomination as an example. I ask you to consider whether there is any valid reason why these various groups should remain apart. We draw our illustration from the Baptist Church. The following are some of its divisions:

Northern Convention
Southern Convention
American Baptist Association
Duck River and kindred associations
Independent Baptist Church of America
The National Convention
The General Six-Principle Baptists
Seventh-Day Baptists
United American Freewill Baptists
Freewill (Bullockite) Baptists
General Baptists
Separate Baptists
Regular Baptists

* Note: Since this sermon was preached, a tenth division has appeared in Presbyterianism.—J. S. B.

Primitive Baptists
Predestinarian Two-Seed-in-the-Spirit Baptists

and so on!

Many of these divisions owe their origin to disputes, on theology or methods of government, that took place possibly a century ago. Five of the divisions in the Presbyterian Church owe their origin to secession movements which took place in the eighteenth or nineteenth century in faraway Scotland. While the grounds of the dispute are today forgotten, the breaches have never been successfully healed.

One writer on the subject of Church union, whose statement I have not been able to verify, declares that in the so-called "Church of God" in this nation there was a conflict some years ago and a branch broke off which called itself "The True Church of God." But even this separated group could not remain at peace, and there developed a third division which called itself "The Only True Church of God."

The problem created by this multitude of divisions within the Protestant Church is not so serious for us in the homelands as it is for the missionary in foreign countries. A native missionary from South India declared: "While unity is a desirable ideal for the Western world, it is vital to the life of the Church in the mission fields." How utterly confusing to the minds of people in non-Christian lands must be our denominational affiliations which are altogether without meaning to them. They seriously retard the progress of the Kingdom of God.

When one speaks of Church union there are people who will say, "I am not prepared to sacrifice the distinctive doctrines of Presbyterianism or of Methodism or Lutheranism," as the case may be; but if you were to ask these people to name to you the doctrines which they are not prepared to relinquish in a union with other Christian bodies, you would find that in ninety-five cases out of a hundred they would be quite unable to identify them.

An interesting illustration of this occurred in the city of Ottawa, Canada, when the movement was under way for the formation of the United Church of Canada. A ministerial friend of mine, very much interested in the consummation of Church union, was a guest at the home of a Presbyterian in Ottawa. In the presence of a number of persons his host said, "My quarrel with this union is the fact that we are asked to surrender the historic doctrines of the Presbyterian Church; and I, for one, consider that these are too precious to be sacrificed."

My friend, who happened to be well qualified in theology, said to the businessman, "I suppose you would recognize the doctrines of the Presbyterian Church if I named them, wouldn't you?" "Why certainly," said this man. "Well," said my friend, "there are five major points in which Calvinism differs from Arminianism. Calvinism, of course, is the basis of Presbyterian theology and Arminianism that of the Methodist Church. Now," said my friend, "I shall name over five doctrines of Calvinism in contrast with the opposing doctrines of Arminianism, and I am going to ask you to choose which you prefer. I shall leave them unnamed, and we shall see how many Calvinistic doctrines you can recognize."

The man made his choice of the five separate alternatives that were offered to him, and, when he had concluded, the minister said, "You have actually chosen four Arminian doctrines and only one Calvinistic. My friend, you are not a Presbyterian at all; you are a Methodist."

It is most certainly not on the basis of the Christian message that Protestants are divided. This fact is borne out by the findings of the Lausanne Conference on Faith and Order in 1927. You recall that eighty-six branches of the Christian Church sent their representatives to that meeting—every major division of Christendom except the Roman Catholic. It was not possible to reach agreement on the nature of the Church or of the Sacraments and some other points, but a basis of practically unanimous agreement was found in the Christian Gospel which the Church has been empowered to proclaim. How significant is that fact! Surely it ought to give us increased hope for the hastening of the day of reunion, which yet must dawn.

Why have many movements for reunion failed in the past? Because we have forgotten the question which the Apostle Paul asked of the people of Corinth: "Is Christ divided?" Only as we make our Lord the center of our allegiance, and not party cries and shibboleths, can reunion be achieved.

Whenever, in the past, Christian leaders have come together to talk about Church union, they have put in the forefront of their discussion questions about the proper forms of Church government; certain methods of celebrating the Holy Communion; endless discussions about clerical orders and methods of Church procedure; but they have failed to give Christ the central place. All these other considerations are secondary to our obligations to him, who is the chief Cornerstone of the Christian Church. The nearer we Christians draw to Christ, the closer we find ourselves to one another.

The Fifth Avenue Presbyterian Church has made a notable contribution to the progress of Church union in this nation. It has demonstrated how precious is the heritage that we have in common. For eight years the Reverend John Henry Jowett exercised a remarkable ministry in this church, and he came here directly from the Congregational Church in Britain. Did anybody feel, during the ministry of Dr. Jowett in New York, that, because he was a Congregationalist, the Gospel that he preached was not acceptable to Presbyterians? I venture to say that no man or woman who came under the influence of Dr. Jowett's ministry ever gave a moment's thought to his denominational affiliations.

My immediate predecessor in this pulpit was the Reverend Henry Howard. Dr. Howard came to this church after a lifelong ministry in the Methodist denomination. Did any Presbyterian in this congregation feel that something was lacking in the Gospel that Dr. Howard preached, because he came from the Methodist Church? To ask the question is to reveal its absurdity.

These preachers of righteousness exercised unforgettable ministries in New York because they exalted Jesus Christ. That was the groundwork upon which they builded, and no other foundation can any man lay. On this basis we must proceed.

Even a cursory examination of the movements

toward Church union that have already taken place in Scotland, England, Canada, and, in the last year or two, in this country also, ought to convince us that the trend toward further division has been definitely arrested. The tide has now turned. In the next quarter of a century, I believe that we shall witness the greatest advance toward the reunion of Protestantism that has taken place since the time of the Reformation.

The history of the Great War affords us a striking illustration of the strategic advantage of unity. On March 26, 1918, the German forces on the Western Front hurled forty-six divisions against one sector of the trenches. They broke through the Allied lines and threatened to drive a wedge between the British and French armies. A desperate crisis had struck. Defeat was staring us in the face. The Allies had more men, more guns, more munitions, more money than the Germans, but they lacked unity. An attempt had been made to merge all the Allied forces under a central command, but jealousy and suspicion on the part of the politicians and military leaders made this impossible.

In the darkest hour of the war came the conference at Doullens. General Pershing, Commander in Chief of the American Army, demanded instant action and offered to put all his troops and materials at the disposal of the Allies. His influence and the imminent peril of the moment achieved what had been impossible up to this time. The Allied forces on the Western Front now became "one front—one army—one nation."

Under the unified command the Belgians struck at

a point in the north, the British at the center of the line; the French advanced in the south; and the American army swept forward on their right. All these efforts were perfectly coordinated. Under the hammer blows of unceasing attacks the enemy line wavered, bent, broke; and his proud battalions were soon scattered in retreat over the broad plains of Flanders and France.

What a lesson this teaches to the Christian Church! She, too, is engaged in a warfare. For nineteen centuries she has been battling against forces of evil strongly entrenched. There are five hundred millions of nominal Christians in the world, but they are more like a rabble than an army. Iniquity is arrogant and defiant. Two-thirds of mankind is yet outside the Christian Church, and the Kingdom still tarries.

Sounding down the centuries comes the ringing message of the Apostle Paul: "Is Christ divided?" It challenges us to demonstrate to the wondering eyes of men that Christianity is the greatest uniting force on earth. May we soon witness a manifestation of the Spirit of God that will bring together the broken and dismembered fragments of his Body and weld them into a glorious Church—a Church which will give its allegiance neither to political dictator nor ecclesiastical potentate, but only to Jesus Christ, its King and Head—a Church that shall stand as the promise and prophecy of the coming of that mighty Kingdom which shall stretch from the river unto the ends of the earth; in which there shall be neither Jew nor Greek, Presbyterian nor Methodist, Episcopalian nor Baptist, bond nor free; but Christ shall be all in all.

OUR PROTESTANT HERITAGE

III. The Rebirth of Protestantism

Then he answered and spake unto me, saying, This is the word of the Lord unto Zerubbabel, saying, Not by might, nor by power, but by my spirit, saith the Lord of hosts.

ZECHARIAH 4:6

ORGANIZED Christianity in America possesses great resources. There are more than two hundred and thirty thousand church edifices in this country valued, with their endowments, at seven billion dollars. Almost one-half of the population are Church members—more than sixty million souls. Since the commencement of this century there has been an uninterrupted increase both in the number of churches and in their membership. From 1900 to 1933 the adult membership increased from twenty-seven millions to more than fifty millions—an advance of 82 per cent, while in the same period the population increase was but 65 per cent. Protestantism has ever been in the van of this forward movement. These facts are cold comfort for the cynics and pessimists who tell us that the Church in America is on the toboggan slide.

But, great as have been the accomplishments of the Christian Church in this nation, its influence has not been commensurate with its numbers or financial resources. The reason is because we are too prone to forget that the Church's effectiveness in any age is dependent not on her material possessions but on the limitless Power of her Lord. I venture to assert that the Church of the first century, deficient in numbers, constantly persecuted, lacking in material riches, yet exerted a mightier spiritual influence than our American Christianity with all its prestige and power.

I am reminded of an incident in the career of Pope Julius II, the Roman Pontiff who increased the Church's wealth and political power but weakened immeasurably its spiritual achievements. One day, from a far-off monastery in Italy, a humble monk came to visit the Pope. He was shown the treasures of literature, art, and sculpture housed in the Vatican. Then Julius II took him to the Church's treasury and showed him heaps of gold and silver that the faithful had donated from various parts of the world. "You see," said Julius, turning to the monk, "the successor of Peter no longer has to say, 'Silver and gold have I none.' " "Aye," responded the monk, "and by the same token neither can he say to the lame man, 'In the name of Jesus Christ of Nazareth rise up and walk.' "

That incident illustrates exactly what I mean. The Church has undeniably increased her material possessions, but she has often done it at the expense of the true riches.

There are always, of course, those croaking spirits in our midst who tell us that the modern world is through with religion; that Christianity will be defeated in the conflict with hostile forces; that the Church is waging a losing battle. No one could tolerate such opinions as these if he believed in God.

We need today the faith of the Prophet Zechariah. A little company of the children of Israel had returned from the exile in Babylon, and amidst discouragement and poverty they attempted to build a humble House of God to take the place of the vanished glories of Solomon's Temple. The hostility of tribes about Jerusalem had stopped building operations for nearly twenty years. "During all that time the hole in the ground, where the foundations had been dug and a few courses of stones lay, gaped desolate, a sad reminder to the feeble band of the failure of their hopes." Some declared that the Temple would never be completed; that theirs was a lost cause. The leader of the Jews, Zerubbabel, was utterly discouraged. It seemed to him that the difficulties in the way towered like a mountain. But the Prophet Zechariah, who possessed an unshakable faith in God, went to Zerubbabel and said: "This is the word of the Lord unto thee: Not by might, nor by power, but by my Spirit, saith the Lord of Hosts Who art thou, O great mountain? before Zerubbabel thou shalt become a plain."

It was not that God's Prophet minimized the difficulties or underrated the opposition, but he knew that the resources of the Eternal God were so great that they could overcome every obstacle, and even mountains would crumble into dust before the hosts of the Lord. The confidence of the Prophet of Israel is akin to that of Jesus, when he says: "If ye have faith as a grain of mustard seed ye shall say unto this mountain:

Remove hence to yonder place; and it shall remove and nothing shall be impossible unto you."

Those who predict failure for the Church in her mission of establishing the Kingdom of God on earth have forgotten the mightiest factor in the whole situation. They have left God out of their reckoning.

When Brennus, the leader of the Gauls, had captured Rome, he offered to retire from the city for a ransom payment of one thousand pounds of gold. As the metal was being weighed in the forum, the Romans complained that the weights were false, whereupon Brennus, the Gallic leader, threw his sword into the scale on top of the weights, crying, "Woe to the vanquished!"

If the Christian Church is dependent upon human plans and human resources, we may well question whether the forces of evil are not too strong for us; but when the Sword of the Lord is thrown into the scale the issue can never again be in doubt. "Not by might, nor by power, but by my Spirit, saith the Lord."

How may we arouse the Church of our Faith to a realization of the infinite resources available to us in God?

First of all, we must restore the Bible to its rightful place in preaching and in private devotions.

Ruskin in *The Stones of Venice* says that the Reformation was in reality a reanimation. As year after year passed into history and the remembrance of the life of Christ sank back into the depths of time, the knowledge of the Bible grew dim and its teachings were obscured in the minds of men and women. Every year "removed the truths of the Gospel into deeper distance and added to them, also, some false or foolish tradition. Then," says Ruskin, "came the Reformation—the reanimated Faith and in its right hand the Book open."

That is a true symbol of the Reformation—"In its right hand the Book open." Protestantism rediscovered a lost Book, lost to priests and people alike. Do you think that it was merely a historical accident that printing by movable type was invented in 1454, and that half a century later there came the Protestant Reformation? There was a time when it took the loving labor of weary months for a scribe to make even one copy of the Scriptures; but the printing press turned out hundreds of copies a day. These Bibles, translated from the Latin and Greek into the language of the common people, poured from the presses by tens of thousands and found their way into the homes of every nation in Europe.

What was the result? J. R. Green in his *History of the English People* tells us of what happened in Britain:

> England became the people of a Book, and that Book was the Bible. It was as yet the one English Book which was familiar to every Englishman; it was read at Churches and read at home, and everywhere its words, as they fell on ears which custom had not deadened to their force and beauty, kindled a startling enthusiasm.

Bishop Bonner set up six of these Bibles in St. Paul's Cathedral. Sunday after Sunday and day after day the crowds gathered in the nave of the church to hear their message read, or hung upon the words of the Geneva Bible as it was read in the devotional exercises at home.

To quote again from Green: "The whole temper of the nation was changed. A new conception of life and of man superseded the old. A new moral and religious impulse spread through every class."

For the privilege of obtaining a few pages of the English Bible in Wycliffe's day, before the invention of printing, men paid large sums of money; and our forefathers willingly yielded up their lives that their children and children's children might not be deprived of this precious heritage. Today that Book can be purchased for the price of admission to a moving-picture show, and there is no individual in all the land, howsoever poor he may be, who cannot obtain a copy of it.

One of the tragedies of our time is the fact that this Book goes unread by multitudes of people, some of whom are yet ready to pay lip service to its greatness. There are few Protestant homes in the length or breadth of this nation in which a copy of the Bible may not be found, but in many of them its function is to lie on some closet shelf where it gathers dust, so that, as Charles Haddon Spurgeon once said, "You could write the word 'damnation' on the cover of it with your finger."

A new day will dawn for the religious life of this nation when our people go back to the practice of reading thoughtfully and earnestly each day a few verses from this Book, in which is recorded the wisdom of the Ages and the Eternities.

And what of the Protestant pulpit? We need more Bible preaching. "The Bible is the preacher's Book and it is the preacher's glory." There is nothing that the minister can say that will carry so much conviction to the heart of his listeners as the authoritative Word of God. In Reformation times great congregations, to whom the Bible was a new and wonderful Book, eagerly listened to its message proclaimed from the pulpits and then went home to search the Scriptures for themselves. I believe that there is a hunger in the hearts of men and women today for the preaching of the Word. Nothing else can give us strength sufficient to meet the sorrows, the temptations, and the trials of life.

If the Protestant pulpit substitutes "topics of the day" for the preaching of the Everlasting Word its ministry must inevitably become sterile and unfruitful. Then we may witness the fulfillment of the warning from Holy Scripture that there will be "a famine in the land: not a famine of bread, nor a thirst for water, but of hearing the Word of the Lord, and they shall wander from sea to sea and from the North even to the East; they shall run to and fro to seek the Word of the Lord and shall not find it." Woe to the nation in which that prophecy will ever find a fulfillment.

As one wise observer has said:

> The preacher is not a public entertainer ministering to the taste of an audience that enjoys fine oratory; he is not a dexterous dairyman skimming the cream of literature and thought and serving it nicely flavoured to dainty consumers—he stands between God and a company of souls whom God created and for whose safe and wise shepherding God will hold him responsible. "Feed my sheep!" "Feed my lambs!" said the Master. . . . So

long as there remains the triple tragedy of sin, suffering and death so long the Bible will speak to the heart of man, and humanity that has once known the Bible will turn away, after the novelty has worn off, from every flashy substitute for the Bible that our modern Athenians push as the latest thing in the spiritual market.

"Not by might, nor by power, but by my Spirit, saith the Lord." The Spirit of God is unfailingly manifested in the preaching of the Word.

If we are going to witness a rebirth of Protestantism in addition to restoring the Bible to its rightful place, we must also call the whole Church to prayer.

Quite frequently today we hear people speak of the need of a revival; and surely American Christianity does stand in need of a spiritual reawakening. A little time ago a minister in the Middle West announced as the topic of his sermon: "Let's Have a Revival." Such an attitude borders almost on presumption. We must never forget that the initiative rests with God.

All religious movements in which deep called unto deep, and new springs of grace were opened in the depth of the soul, originated in special action on God's part. Human effort apart from the Divine Initiative has always been abortive, as many withered expectations in all our experiences show.

When the fervor of spiritual renewal is kindled afresh in thousands of hearts it will not be the result of our plans, our resources, our crusades, but it will be because of a Divine Visitation. "Not by might, nor by power, but by my Spirit, saith the Lord of Hosts."

We have seen, however, that a primary requisite for the outpouring of God's Spirit is the cooperation of his people. As the Spirit of God is revealed through the Bible so his Power is released in prayer. In the spiritual realm God's methods are not different from his operations in all other spheres of human endeavor. All the energy that the farmer uses in tilling the soil and preparing it for the seed is only 5 per cent of the total energy necessary for the growing of a crop; but man's 5-per-cent cooperation is essential to his receiving the 95 per cent of God's response.

So it is in the realms of science, whether of physics, medicine, astronomy, or any other branch. God does not blazon his laws out on the heavens so that his gifts may be obtained without any effort on man's part; but it is only as a Pasteur, a Lister, a Marconi, an Edison, a Pupin cooperates with God in self-forgetting labors that he reveals his wonders to man.

In the spiritual realm God's power is released through the intercession of his people. The Bible and Christian history testify to the truth of this: Moses at the burning bush, Amos in the wilderness with his flocks and herds, Isaiah in the temple, Luther in his monastery cell, Wesley in the Moravian prayer meeting. One by one God called these men, coming to them in unexpected ways; endowing them with his own power and sending them forth as irresistible messengers of his Truth.

Dwight L. Moody declared that this was the source of the power that accompanied his preaching. He tells us about his efforts in a Chicago church. In spite of the earnestness with which he delivered his sermons the expected results did not come. He noticed one Sunday that some women seated near the front of the church were praying throughout the service. At the close he went to them and asked, "For whom are you praying?" They replied, "We are praying for you." "Well," said Moody, "I want you to pray for the people rather than for me. They are the ones who need your prayers." But they replied, "No, we are going to keep on praying for you until God's power will be given to you."

After some months passed the day of power came. Let me quote from Moody's own words:

> One day in the city of New York— Ah, what a day; I cannot describe it. I seldom refer to it. It is almost too sacred an experience to name—Paul had an experience of which he did not speak for fourteen years—I can only say God revealed Himself to me, and I had such an experience of His love that I had to ask Him to stay His Hand. I went to preach again. The sermons were not different; I did not present any new truths; and yet hundreds were converted.

Out of that experience stepped forth the Dwight L. Moody who first in London and later in New York shook the world.

That power is available to us. God has set this Church in the midst of a mighty city where we can feel the heart throbs of the Western world. Here is an unparalleled opportunity and an equally great responsibility. Already God has blessed us, but that which we have experienced is only a foretaste of what he has in store for us. We must give ourselves unceasingly to the ministry of prayer. It may be that

God will use this Church as the instrument of a spiritual awakening which, beginning here, will be felt throughout the length and breadth of the land.

A door of opportunity is flung wide open, and there are many adversaries. But the mountains of difficulty will become as a plain, for our trust is not in material resources or organizations, but in Him alone who said, "Not by might, nor by power, but by my spirit."

"IS MORALITY BREAKING DOWN?"

He gave them their request; but sent leanness into their soul.

PSALMS 106:15

He let them have what they desired, then—made them loathe it.

MOFFATT'S TRANSLATION

OUR text is from Psalm 106, verse 15: "He gave them their request; but sent leanness into their soul." That is the rendering of the Authorized Version. The Hebrew word "razon" translated "leanness" means literally "loathing." Moffatt's translation puts it: "He let them have what they desired, then—made them loathe it."

"He let them have what they desired." That assertion implies that God answers prayer. But the prayer which he answers is not, necessarily, the spoken word. Sometimes our truest prayer is not uttered at all. It expresses itself in the desire of our hearts—a passionate craving that, perhaps, we would not dare to express in our prayers.

The facts of life would indicate that men and women usually achieve the goal of their desires. If they set their hearts on a thing, generally they get it.

That is natural, because a strong craving for something coordinates all our powers for the attainment of the desired object.

A young man, for instance, determines, on the very threshold of life, that money-making will be his goal. That will be the one insistent demand that he will make on life. The chances are that he will succeed. All his faculties will be trained to work toward the one end. His wits will be sharpened. His powers of acquisitiveness will be heightened. His cupidity will be increased. He will count no labor too hard or no association too debasing that will achieve the goal of his dominant desire. Instinctively he will draw about him people who can further the ends he has in view. He will find, of course, that his lust for gold has blinded his eyes to many of the richest gifts of God. Nevertheless, he will get his request.

That is true, also, in the life of the individual who desires illicit pleasures. No sooner has that become the compelling urge of his life than all the base things in the world will begin to minister to him. Evil companions become his friends. Literature that the healthy-minded man disregards stretches out eager hands to him. He is attracted by the unwholesome as steel filings are drawn by a magnet. His desires are driven by one impulse, and that impulse creates a vacuum which sucks into itself everything that degrades and defiles. He will get his request.

But, says the Psalmist, these people whose ideals are pitched low have no sooner had their prayers answered and their desires satisfied than they begin to loathe the thing which formerly they had craved. The Bible illustrates that truth. You recall how Lot, the nephew of Abraham, hungered for the wealth and the pleasures of Sodom, and he got them, but, with them, he got Sodom's pollution. King Ahab coveted Naboth's vineyard. He wanted it so badly that he got it. But retribution followed on his achievement.

The young man Samson wanted Delilah. He got her. But the gift brought him blindness and degrading servitude as a slave of the Philistines.

Judas wanted a handful of silver, and he got it; but, with it, he got a suicide's grave.

Some of the greatest tragedies in life have been brought about by the fulfillment of dominant desires, for, in the words of the Psalmist, "He gave them their request, then—made them loathe it."

Our text written centuries ago is fulfilled today in the experience of the moral cynics. We are hearing a lot about the "new morality." It purports to lead mankind from inhibitions and restrictions into glorious freedom. Most of the advocates of this cult have succeeded, to their own satisfaction at least, in getting rid of God, and now they are going to get rid of morals.

The postwar period in every part of the world ushered in a time of widespread disillusionment and cynicism. The severe restraint that had been imposed upon people during the years of that colossal struggle, with its discipline, its wounds, its death, had at last been released, and the pendulum swung far in the opposite direction.

A school of writers appeared on the scene, and they enriched themselves by exploiting a morality which glorified the libertine, sneered at virtue, and exalted licentiousness. "The greatest need of people," they said, "is self-expression: the ability to cast aside the outworn bonds of self-control that have too long inhibited our lives. Morals, as the origin of the word reveals, are nothing more than conventions that change with every generation. There is no such thing as unalterable moral standards. Goodness, virtue, purity, are passing phases in public thought, a matter of taste like fashions in clothes. Morality is only what the neighbors think."

But some people protested, "What is going to happen to the standards of morality upon which the social life of our nation is based? What is going to happen to the home and family life, if all fidelity and self-control is swept away?" The answer of the moral sophisticates is quite clear. "Nothing," they say, "should be allowed to interfere with the freedom of sex life. If the ideals of family life stand in the way of this freedom, the family must be mended or ended."

Unfortunately, there were not a few people who took these prophets of the "new morality" at their word. The result has been the moral shipwreck of many lives and the breakup of many homes.

The public taste, satiated and not a little disgusted, is turning away now from this type of literature, but it has left its stamp upon the minds of thousands of young people in our time.

The first thing that we have to say about the "new morality" is that it is not new at all. It is as old as the human race. You will find it among the ancient Greeks and Romans, who took the philosophy of Epicurus, with its emphasis on pleasure, and applied it in directions to which he had never intended it should go. Self-expression was carried to utter extremes, and there resulted a wave of unbridled licentiousness which ate into the character of these peoples and, finally, brought the downfall of two mighty empires.

Matthew Arnold, writing of that period, says:

> On that hard pagan world disgust
> And secret loathing fell.
> Deep weariness and sated lust
> Made human life a hell.

"He gave them their request; but sent loathing into their souls."

The overemphasis of self-expression appeared again at the time of the Renaissance. For centuries before there had been asceticism, restraint, repression, but all these restricting bonds were broken in the rush of new life released in the rediscovery of art, sculpture, and literature, in fifteenth-century Italy. The splendid achievement in these spheres, unfortunately, went hand in hand with a corruption of morals. Self-control was a subject of jest.

The moral depths to which men sank is illustrated in the life of Lorenzo "*il Magnifico*"—Lorenzo "the Magnificent"—the ruler of Florence near the close of the fifteenth century. A patron of art and letters, he was also a patron of vice in its most degrading forms, and he led his people into ever-new debaucheries. As one has put it: "The brilliance of the Renaissance was the brilliance of the surface of a stagnant pool which conceals the foulness beneath."

The swing of the pendulum from self-restraint to self-expression is seen, again, in the Restoration in

England, when Charles II came to the throne. Once more we have the illustration of a ruler inciting his people to unblushing profligacy. Charles spent the greater part of his time, as J. R. Green has said, "either gambling in the Newmarket, or toying with his mistresses at Whitehall."

So there you are: the "new morality" is not new at all. It was practiced in Sodom, in Babylon, in Athens, in Rome, in Britain, and other countries, wherever there were found men and women willing to follow this mirage, which unfailingly reveals itself in disillusionment and bitterness of soul.

Even the most extreme of modern sophisticates cannot produce one sin that is new and that has not been worn threadbare through the centuries. They are all catalogued in the first chapter of Paul's Epistle to the Romans. It has been true of the moral cynics in every age that "He gave them their request, then—made them loathe it."

The writer who has probably made a deeper impression than any other in the teaching of moral revolt is Mr. Bertrand Russell of England. In his book *Marriage and Morals* he tells us quite frankly that the only way to achieve a stable married life is to dismiss fidelity altogether, to allow it no claims whatsoever. Only by giving to each party of the marriage vow complete freedom can there be any permanency in the relationship. His wife, Mrs. Russell, in her book *The Right to Be Happy,* argues for the same viewpoint.

Surely, then, when both husband and wife believe in the philosophy of infidelity, we ought to have, in their married life, an example of supreme happiness.

The contrary, however, has been the case. When I was last in England, a little more than a year ago, one of the most disgusting divorce trials in the history of that nation was under way, so that Bertrand Russell and his wife might be able to gain their freedom from each other. Their much-vaunted infidelity had failed to achieve its purpose.

George Arnold, in his poem "The Lees of Life," summarizes in a vivid fashion the experience of people like the Russells, who have found in the "devaluated pleasures" of life nothing but emptiness and insipidity. He says:

I have had my will,
  Tasted every pleasure,
I have drunk my fill
  Of the purple measure.
Life has lost its zest,
Sorrow is my guest,
  O, the lees are bitter, bitter!
Give me rest!

Love once filled the bowl,
  Running o'er with blisses,
Made my very soul
  Drunk with crimson kisses.
But I drank it dry,
Love has passed me by
  O, the lees are bitter, bitter!
Let me die!

"He gave them their request; but sent loathing into their souls."

Let no one persuade you, however, that religion is

opposed to self-expression; that it "pushes in the stops and shuts off the rich full music of life." It was Jesus who said: "I am come that they might have life, and that they might have it more abundantly." The Greek ideal was beauty. The Hebrew ideal was holiness. But these two conceptions reach a perfect unity in the quality of life into which Christ leads men—the beauty of holiness. Self-expression and self-control unite in a glorious synthesis in Christian character.

The Christian ideal, I am willing to admit, is not easy of attainment. We humans, torn by wayward passions, find it difficult to walk that white highway. The reason why many people fail morally is because they have lost faith in God. That is the foundation of Bertrand Russell's moral cynicism. Long ago he had cast aside belief in God, and faith in a moral order very soon followed. As Will Durant has well said: "Morality without God is as weak as a traffic law when the policeman is on foot."

The basis of our faith in the eternity of moral values rests foursquare upon our belief in God, who is the Upholder of the moral order. The individual today who seeks to triumph amid all the temptations and bewilderments of modern life will need the reenforcement of that Divine Power which will enable him "to expel the coward and enthrone the hero that is in the heart of every man." He will need the undergirding strength of God.

Can you conceive of anything more thrilling, more adventurous, more replete with romance than a genuine experience of love, untarnished by lust; of marriage, a home, children, and an affection that deepens as the years go by? All the promises of moral sophistication are but a drab and colorless caricature of this glorious reality.

I talked some years ago with a dear old couple who were celebrating the sixtieth anniversary of their wedding. I quoted to them the words of Mark Twain, where he said: "You have got to be married for a quarter of a century before you know the meaning of true love." In reply, my friend put his arm tenderly round his wife, who had journeyed with him on so long a pilgrimage, and, with a quiet smile, he said: "Mark Twain didn't know anything about it. You have got to be married for sixty years before you know the meaning of love."

How beautiful it is to see two souls like these, perfectly joined together, having come through dark days and bright days, always bearing and sharing each other's sorrows and joys, and entering into an ever-deepening intimacy as the years pass by.

When the *Titanic* was speeding across the Atlantic Ocean in April, 1912, on her maiden voyage, suddenly and without any warning, the deadly spur of a submerged iceberg tore into her hull, and ripped it open under the water for a distance of three hundred feet. More than twenty-three hundred people had come face to face with death. All the lifeboats and rafts could accommodate only eleven hundred. On the passenger decks, from the bottom to the top, there was heartbreaking bravery and some quite understandable cowardice. The last distress signal was fired in vain. An officer stood by the rail and urged the women and children forward. "Ladies," he said insistently, "you must get in at once. There's not a minute to lose. Hurry. Get in. Get in." He seized the arm of little old Mrs. Isidore Strauss of New York and pushed her toward the lifeboat. She looked appealingly at the officer and glanced toward her husband; but the officer cried, "The men must stand back. Women and children first. Hurry on, lady, hurry on." Without a moment's hesitation, Mrs. Strauss stepped away from the lifeboat, spurning the opportunity of rescue, and, going to the side of her husband, from whom she had never been separated from the time of their marriage, she took his hand, and twenty minutes later, locked in each other's arms, they went down into the cold waters of the Atlantic. As they had been joined together in life, in death they were not divided.

Choose you this day which way ye shall take: "the way that seemeth right unto a man, the end of which is death"; or "the path of the just, which is as a shining light that shineth more and more unto the perfect day."

To every man there openeth
A way, and ways, and a way,
And the high soul climbs the high way,
And the low soul gropes the low;
And in between, on the misty flats,
The rest drift to and fro.
But to every man there openeth
A high way and a low,
And every man decideth
The way his soul shall go.

THE VALLEY OF INDECISION

And Elijah came unto all the people, and said, How long halt ye between two opinions? if the Lord be God, follow him; but if Baal, then follow him.

I KINGS 18:21

THERE are some texts in the Bible that sound a wooing note drawing us as tenderly as the hands of a mother: "Come unto me all ye that labor and are heavy laden, and I will give you rest."

There are other texts that breathe a spirit of calm and peace, like quiet waters at eventide: "The Lord is my shepherd; I shall not want. He maketh me to lie down in green pastures: he leadeth me beside the still waters."

There are still other texts that rouse us like the blast of a trumpet, and the one we are studying today comes into the third category: "How long halt ye between two opinions? If the Lord be God, follow him; but if Baal, then follow him."

"How long halt ye?" The word "halt" in the original Hebrew means literally "to go lame" or "to limp." So what Elijah is saying to the people of Israel is this: "How long go ye limping between the two sides? Come to a decision and act on it. If the Lord be God, follow him; but if Baal, then follow him."

This text forms a part of one of the most dramatic incidents in the Bible. It might be called "The Battle of the Gods." The scene is set on Mount Carmel, that majestic mountain which rises sixteen hundred feet above the level of the sea, and from whose summit can be seen, far off to the West, the rolling waters of the Mediterranean. The people are gathered on a plateau or tableland, high up on the mountain. The multitude of Israel is there, with Ahab the King and his wife Jezebel. With him are ranged eight hundred and fifty prophets of Baal. On the opposite side stands the prophet Elijah—stern, solitary, majestic!

What is the meaning of this amazing congress? What are all these heathen priests doing in Israel? Above all, why is yonder altar of Jehovah broken down, grass grown, abandoned? Israel has fallen on evil days. Ahab, brave and impetuous, a builder of cities, a king who advanced the material fortunes of the children of Israel, has made a grievous blunder. He formed an alliance with Itto-Baal, King of Tyre, and cemented that alliance by marrying Jezebel, the daughter of Itto-Baal.

This Phoenician queen brought to the Israelites no little sense of pride. She brought riches, pomp, prestige, and all the luxuries of Oriental royalty; but with these material advantages she brought also corruption, immorality, idolatry. It could not be otherwise. Her father, Itto-Baal, King of Tyre, was a bloodthirsty tyrant. He had no right to the throne of Tyre. He was an usurper.

Itto-Baal had been High Priest in the Temple of

Ashtoreth in Tyre. Ashtoreth was a female deity who exercised a degrading influence upon her worshipers. She, with Baal, was venerated by the Phoenicians. Itto-Baal was actually the High Priest of Tyre. The real King was Phelles, the brother of Itto-Baal. But Itto-Baal plotted against his brother and, when the time was opportune, murdered him. He took the throne in his stead. It was this King, Itto-Baal, who made an alliance with Ahab of Israel. That bloody man was the father of Jezebel, and she was his true daughter.

No sooner had Jezebel married Ahab than she and her father determined that they would plant their own religion in the soil of Israel. Before long Jezebel had her way. She has ever been regarded as one of the most notorious women of history—implacable, imperious, indomitable—as cruel as her father. The proof of that can be seen in an event recorded in the Book of Kings. Jezebel successfully plotted the murder of Naboth, one of her subjects, in order to obtain his vineyard. She was indeed her father's daughter. Her hands, too, were dyed in human blood.

When we think of Jezebel we are reminded of Catherine de Medici of France. The historian says that her statesmanship was based upon finesse, lying, and assassination. When Catherine saw the power of the Protestants increasing in France, she plotted the death, by murder, of Admiral Coligny, one of their leaders. Following hard upon the wake of that crime, she instituted the Massacre of Saint Bartholomew by which, in one night, thirty thousand Protestants were slain in France. That ghastly deed has ever been laid directly at the door of Catherine de Medici. She was another Jezebel.

Jezebel had her counterpart, too, in Empress Irene, head of the Eastern Roman Empire in Constantinople. The Empress ruled her subjects with a rod of iron. She was vain, dictatorial, pitiless. When her son came of age and began to reign she plotted against him and overthrew him. He was brought a prisoner to her palace in Constantinople. In the presence of his mother and at her express command, his eyes were stabbed out.

Jezebel was Catherine de Medici and Empress Irene rolled into one. For a thousand years her name was a byword in the land of Israel. She was not satisfied merely with the worship of Baal in her new kingdom. At her instigation a magnificent temple was built to this heathen deity. It was served by eight hundred and fifty priests who ate, amid luxury, at her table. They celebrated their religious rites with costly vessels and pompous ritual, and, little by little, the worship of Jehovah declined.

But even this did not satisfy Jezebel. She started a campaign of persecution and broke down all the altars of Jehovah. Not even the lone altar on Mount Carmel escaped her eagle eye.

Then followed the extermination of the prophets of Jehovah. Ahab, instead of opposing his wife, weakly submits to this bloody campaign.

In the very moment that Jezebel congratulates herself on having completed the conquest of Israel's God her peace is disturbed. Like a comet flaming in the midnight sky, Elijah suddenly appears again.

"Art thou he that troubleth Israel?" asks the indignant Ahab. "Nay," replied Elijah, "I have not troubled Israel, but thou and thy father's house, in that ye have forsaken the commandments of the Lord, and thou hast followed Baalim."

Ahab has met his match. Elijah does not cringe before the King. He does not wear courtly garments. He is clad in camel's hair, with a leather girdle about his loins. He is not begging favors. He does not kneel in the presence of royalty. He stands there as an equal, nay, as a superior, for he is the Prophet of the living God. "Elijah has spent too long a time in the ravines and barren uplands of Gilead to tremble in the presence of any man. In those lonely solitudes he has learned to fear man little, because he fears God much." He delivers his message. It is a challenge to all the prophets of Baal, and to their god, as well.

All Israel is now summoned to Mount Carmel. On the one side stand the King and Queen and the serried ranks of the prophets of Baal. On the other side Elijah stands alone. The people are gathered in a dense mass in the foreground. Nearby can be seen the broken-down, abandoned altar of Jehovah.

To the assembled nation Elijah delivers his challenge. It is like the blast of a trumpet—clear, decisive, unequivocal. "How long go ye limping between the two sides? If Jehovah be God, follow him; but if Baal, then follow him." There is scorn and biting sarcasm in Elijah's question.

The shaft went right into the heart of King Ahab. He has been limping between the two sides. While he consents to Jezebel's campaign for the extermination of the religion of Jehovah, he pays deference to the God of his fathers by calling his children after him.

The name of one of his sons was "Ahaziah," which means "Jehovah supports." So Ahab does obeisance to Jehovah, while he follows the whims of the heathen Jezebel. He is trying to serve two masters.

But if the people of Israel cannot know where Ahab stands, there is no doubt as to Elijah's convictions. It must have shamed Ahab even to hear the Prophet pronounce his name. In the Hebrew, "Elijah" is "Elijahu," which means "Jehovah is my God." How it thrills us to meet a man like the Prophet Elijah—fearless, unwavering, determined. "Stop trying to be neutral," says Elijah. "You cannot serve two masters. Why go limping between the two sides? If Jehovah be God, follow him; but if Baal, then follow him."

We learn from the Book of Kings that, at the very moment when Elijah stood alone, there were actually seven thousand in Israel who had not bowed the knee to Baal and whose lips had not kissed his image. Where were the seven thousand? Why was the Prophet of the living God standing alone? The reason is painfully evident. They were afraid! They did not dare to let the world know where they stood. Their lives were dominated by cowardice. Only one man in Israel was found unflinchingly on the side of Jehovah.

It is a long way back to the day when the summons of our text was uttered by one of the prophets of Israel. A similar challenge is needed, however, in our own time, for there are multitudes of people who are living in the valley of indecision. In their heart of hearts they know that they believe in God. But they are afraid to confess him. They are dubious, hesitant, vacillating. Almost as many such people can be found within the Christian Church as outside it. Nobody can be sure just where they stand.

One reason why the Kingdom of God tarries in our day is because so many who have named the name of Christ are either afraid, or ashamed, to show their colors. There are millions of Christians in the modern world whose life and whose influence is not counting in the struggle of right against wrong. They are Christians in name alone.

That spirit is far removed from the heroism of first-century Christianity. In the Book of the Acts we read that the apostles were arrested by the Jerusalem authorities and severely beaten. When at last they were released it was with the express command that they should not speak in the name of Jesus. Then follow these stirring words: "And they departed from the presence of the council rejoicing that they were counted worthy to suffer shame for his name. And daily in the temple and in every house they ceased not to teach and preach Jesus Christ."

A few hundred Christians with a faith as resolute and dauntless as that would stir this great city to its foundations. But what happens today? Go into a drawing room or into a club and listen to the conversation. At one moment the subject is politics, then economics, now the international situation. Practically everybody there is willing to take a decisive stand on any of these issues. They set forth clear-cut views and are unashamed of their convictions. But mention the subject of religion and a strange silence falls upon the company. Everyone suddenly becomes dumb or apologetic.

Why should we hesitate to affirm our faith, even in

circles where it is challenged? If we believe in God, why not say so? If we believe that the establishment of his Kingdom would bring a better world, why should we not declare that conviction?

One of the tragedies of organized religion in our day is that "God lacks courageous, convinced, outspoken witnesses—men and women who have a faith that is not only vital, but is also vocal." The Psalmist voiced an urgent need when he said: "Let the redeemed of the Lord say so." And Isaiah spoke a brave word to the people of his day when he urged them to lift up their voice "like a trumpet." That is the note that the world is waiting for, the note of a trumpet—decisive, arresting, positive, challenging, defiant! That is the kind of testimony that God desires. Like a trumpet? There are multitudes of modern Christians who fear to lift up their voices even like a piccolo.

The Bible is stern in its condemnation of those who seek to be neutrals in a moral conflict. "No man," says Jesus, "can serve two masters." There is no use trying to compromise. You will either love the one and hate the other, or else you will give your allegiance to one and spurn the other. "Ye cannot serve God and Mammon." It is impossible to take a middle position. "He that is not with me is against me, and he that gathereth not with me, scattereth abroad."

In the Book of the Revelation is a message addressed to the Church of Laodicea—the Church that tried to play the rôle of neutral. "I know thy works," says God, "that thou art neither cold nor hot, and because thou art lukewarm, and neither cold nor hot,

I will spew thee out of my mouth." That Church was rejected because it lacked the moral courage to take a decided stand for righteousness.

"How long," asks Elijah in derision, "will ye go limping between the two sides? If Jehovah be God, follow him." There are two reasons why there ought to be no doubt as to where we stand on these matters. First of all, for our own sake. Nothing creates self-confidence and banishes uncertainty so quickly as a decisive, resolute stand. The reason many people turn their backs upon high decisions which they once made is that they have left the door wide open for such a retreat. They have not declared themselves.

The moral conflict in the life of many a young man and woman would be less severe if those who associate with them knew where they stood; if it were known that they would neither retreat nor compromise. Cross the Rubicon. Burn the bridges behind you. Make no provision for a relapse. Don't limp any longer between the two sides. Say within your soul, "I believe in God, and I shall carry that conviction down into every area of my daily life. I shall never be ashamed to let people know where I stand."

In the second place we ought to take a decisive stand for the sake of the Kingdom of God. There were seven thousand, in Israel, who had not bowed the knee to Baal, but they were of little use to the Kingdom because they were afraid to declare themselves.

This was true also of Jesus' day. Even among the rulers, the Scripture tells us, there were many who believed in the Master but they were afraid to confess him lest they should be put out of the synagogues. They were disciples in secret. Nicodemus, creeping out to Jesus under cover of darkness, was one of these. He left the Master standing alone in the hour of his trial and death. Think what it would have meant to his cause, if some of these secret believers had arisen, in the Sanhedrin, and declared, "I, for one, believe in the Nazarene." It might have turned the tide in his favor. But they were afraid, so they failed him.

Look out over this broken, sinful world, with its fears and its hates, its lust and its greed, its exploitation of man by man, and ask yourself this question, "Is there any other way to save it than the way that Jesus Christ has shown? Is there any hope for man other than the living God?" If you believe that his way is the only way, what are you doing about it? There are Christian Churches bravely trying to hold aloft the Cross of Christ in this great city. Is your life counting for him in one of them? Are you helping in some young people's organization, or in a Sunday school where little ones are learning to know the Master? Is your influence felt by your associates in business and in professional life? Have you enlisted in the great Crusade for the overthrow of age-old evils and the establishment of righteousness? Or are you one of those who limp between the two sides?

What a pity that anyone who has ever named the name of Christ should be willing "to allow the case for him to go by default." Do you recall the words of Jesus, vibrant with insistent warning: "Whosoever, therefore, shall be ashamed of me, and of my words, in this adulterous and sinful generation, of him will the Son of Man be ashamed in the presence of his Father and the holy angels."

I challenge you, now, to invest your life in the service of the Church of Jesus Christ and, through it, in the service of him who is its King and Head. Cease limping between the two sides. Come to a decision and abide by it to the end. "If the Lord be God, follow him."

He is sounding forth the trumpet that shall never call retreat.
He is sifting out the hearts of men before his judgment seat.
O, be swift, my soul, to answer him, be jubilant, my feet.
Our God is marching on!

A PROTESTANT VIEW OF THE CONFESSIONAL

Confess your faults one to another, and pray one for another, that ye may be healed. The effectual fervent prayer of a righteous man availeth much.

JAMES 5:16

IN THE last quarter of a century we have been witnessing a retreat from the Reformation. The belated discovery has been made that in all revolutions, whether political or religious, the extremist comes into his own. The Protestant Reformation has not been an exception. So eager were some of its adherents to sweep away every vestige of "Popery" that they sometimes cast into the discard institutions and practices which, through the centuries, have demonstrated their value in the Christian Church.

It is natural and inevitable, therefore, that eventually there should be a reaction. One of the evidences of this is the recognition of the place of beauty in worship. Gothic architecture is regaining its former preeminence. We no longer believe that the ends of religion are served by breaking priceless windows in cathedrals. Protestantism, as well as Catholicism, is using the resources of ecclesiastical art and architecture to stimulate the spirit of worship. We are sure that beauty and holiness are not mutually exclusive.

Indeed some Protestant clergymen are so carried away by their zeal for pre-Reformation practices that they are now telling us that the Reformation was a mistake, that it was nothing short of a tragedy, and that the only hope for the Christian world in the future lies in retracing our steps and seeking reunion with Rome.

The Anglo-Catholic party in the Episcopal Church has oftentimes upheld this viewpoint and has labored unceasingly to bring back into Protestant churches ceremonies that were abolished at the time of the Reformation. Among the institutions reestablished is the confessional. I have visited Episcopal churches in various parts of Great Britain and America and have observed confessional booths bearing notices of the hours at which confessions will be heard. There is nothing in the outward appearance of these booths to differentiate them from the ones which may be seen in every Roman Catholic Church.

Now I suppose that most Protestants are sufficiently broad minded to admit that there must be some elements of value in an institution, like the confessional, which has persisted through the centuries. If that were not so it would never have survived. Should we not then attempt to discover this abiding reality and apply it in our own religious faith?

Undoubtedly the reason that confession makes such a strong appeal to many people is because it affords them an opportunity to unburden their hearts to someone who will keep inviolate the confidences they offer. At times the mental strain of a secret sin or an unadjusted problem becomes almost unbearable. The relief afforded by a full confession is great beyond telling.

Should we then seek to restore, in our Protestant churches, the Roman confessional? By no means! It was a sound instinct that guided the leaders of the Reformation in their rejection of this institution.

The Roman confessional is based on the teaching that Almighty God has conferred upon certain officials of the Christian Church the power of extending or withholding his grace. That doctrine in its extreme form may be seen in the Interdict. By a stroke of the pen Pope Innocent III forbade all celebration of public worship, all administration of the Sacraments, and the use of the burial service in two great countries of Europe. The Interdict was applied in France in the year 1200 and in England in 1209. It was feared more than the Black Death. It is significant that there is no record of its application to any nation since the time of the Reformation and there is little likelihood that we shall ever see it invoked again.

The unique claims of the Church of Rome as manifested in the Interdict have persisted, in a less pronounced form, in the confessional. There are six commandments of the Roman Church, the third of which is that the faithful must make a good confession at least once a year. An annual confession and Communion is the minimum requirement that will keep a Roman Catholic in good standing with his Church.

By no possibility can he fulfill his duties by making confession to God. It must be made to a priest because, according to the teaching of his Church, the forgiveness of God is mediated through the priesthood.

"Can the priest forgive sins?" asks the Roman Catholic catechism. It then answers the question as follows: "Yes, the priest can forgive sins by the power of God."

Now if we Protestants were to admit this Roman doctrine then indeed should we be playing traitor to the Reformation and disregarding its fundamental principle. The basic doctrine of Protestantism is "the priesthood of all believers," which teaches that the humblest Christian can approach the throne of God for his grace and forgiveness without the intervention of priest or minister.

It is true that St. James, addressing his fellow Christians, says: "Confess your faults one to another, and pray one for another. . . ." The Roman Catholic Cardinal Cajetan admits that this verse does not refer to auricular confession but is rather "a mutual admission of special faults." The confession here referred to is not by a penitent to a priest but rather by two Christians to each other. No mention is made of apostles, bishops, or priests but only of "a righteous man." In our text St. James suggests that if there be a burden of guilt weighing upon the conscience it may help greatly to talk the matter over with some good Christian man. Then as our prayers mingle before the Throne of Grace the realization of God's forgiveness will come stealing into our hearts. Many people, not excluding Church members, find no little satisfaction in discussing the faults of other people. It might be a salutary experience then for them occasionally to spend some time confessing their own.

Although Protestantism stands unalterably opposed to a system of auricular confession that is habitual and compulsory and that is based on the teaching that forgiveness may be obtained only through a sacerdotal priesthood, nevertheless it leaves the door wide open, as our text makes clear, for confession that is occasional and voluntary.

The time has come for Protestant people—and especially Protestant ministers—to realize that here is a vitally important and helpful ministry which has all too largely been surrendered since the Reformation. Our Protestant faith will be enriched and made more effective in the lives of our people when we reëmphasize the value of confession to God, in the presence of an understanding Christian or, still better, in the presence of a Christian minister; for he—by his training and experience—is best fitted to offer consolation and advice and—by his ordination vows—is pledged to keep inviolate the confidences that are intrusted to him.

The Bible does not stand alone in urging confession of sin. Some of the best minds among the psychiatrists and psychologists of our time emphasize the therapeutic value of a cleansing religious experience. Dr. C. G. Jung of Switzerland, in his book *Modern Man in Search of a Soul,* states his conviction that the Protestant ministry of today stands on the verge of a vast horizon of effective service but seems not to have noticed it. He suggests that many people might be saved from nervous disorders, and even physical and mental breakdown, were they dealt with understandingly by ministers, in personal interviews. Dr. Jung records his own experience in this regard:

> During the past thirty years people from all the civilized countries of the earth have consulted me. . . . Among all my patients in the second half of life—that is to say, those over thirty-five—there has not been one whose problem in the last resort was not that of finding a religious outlook on life. It is safe to say that every one of them fell ill because he had lost that which the living religions of every age have given to their followers, and none of them has been really healed who did not regain his religious outlook.

Dr. John Rathbone Oliver of Johns Hopkins University, one of the pioneer psychiatrists of America, is in full accord with Dr. Jung in his estimate of the part that religion plays in the maintenance of mental and physical health. Dr. Oliver stresses especially confession.

Only a few weeks ago a medical doctor with a wide practice in New York said to me: "The ministers of New York are missing a great opportunity. Scores of people are flocking to the doctors with problems that are basically religious. Clergymen could deal much more effectively with them than we, but these people believe that ministers would not welcome their confidences."

Here, surely, is a situation that the Protestant Church ought frankly to face.

Why do psychiatrists and medical practitioners lay so much stress on the inner life of people and emphasize so insistently the value of consultation and, if necessary, confession? The reason, I think, is because of our increasing knowledge of the subconscious mind. Every student of psychology is familiar with the term, "subliminal consciousness." "Subliminal" literally means "under the threshold." The subliminal consciousness is that area which lies below the threshold of the consciousness. In the subconscious mind there are buried memories of the past, some happy and some intensely tragic.

"Old, unhappy, far-off things."

From the depths of the subconscious life there sometimes arise memories, emotions, impulses that express themselves in the conscious life of the individual, like bubbles that arise from the bed of a millpond and break upon the surface. They make their presence known in acute nervous disorders, decreasing efficiency in daily tasks, a sense of inferiority, phobias, and mental anguish that destroys the peace of mind and heart. The more he strives to repress these memories that cry out for a hearing the worse does the nervous condition of the patient become.

In every case where the trouble is due to past transgressions the sovereign remedy is a full and complete confession. That alone can bring the realization of God's forgiveness, with inward cleansing and peace.

Shakespeare, who plumbed the depths of human emotions, understood how desperate may be this need. In his tragedy *Macbeth* we see Lady Macbeth, after the murder of Duncan, King of Scotland, tortured by a guilty conscience. In her dreams, where the subconscious mind holds sway, she sees again the stain of the dead king's blood on her hands. She walks in her sleep, frantically trying to efface this evidence of her guilt.

> Out, damned spot! Out, I say! . . . . .
> Here's the smell of blood still;
> All the perfumes of Arabia will not sweeten this
> little hand.

Macbeth, who has been watching his wife, says to the attendant physician:

> Canst thou not minister to a mind diseas'd,
> Pluck from the memory a rooted sorrow,
> Raze out the written troubles of the brain,
> And with some sweet oblivious antidote
> Cleanse the stuff'd bosom of that perilous stuff
> Which weighs upon the heart?

To which the physician replies:

> Therein the patient must minister to himself.

The great dramatist was right. Each of us holds in his hand the key to his own happiness. Only he can unlock the secret door that allows the peace of God to enter and find a dwelling place in his heart.

It was a need similar to this of which St. James was thinking when he penned our text: "Confess your faults one to another, and pray one for another, that ye may be healed. The effectual fervent prayer of a righteous man availeth much."

Any minister who has looked deep into human hearts will not be deluded, by the placid exterior of men and women, into thinking that few people have problems to distress them. He has learned, from experience, that in a multitude of human lives there is restlessness, nervous tension, inner confusion, and disintegration of character. He knows too that to him has been intrusted a message that can bring into these disoriented lives healing, serenity, and peace.

From scores of cases I shall select one that is typical. About two months ago there came to my study a young man in deep distress. He was in his twenties. He had been married for about four years and was living in New York. One could see at a glance that he was laboring under a terrific nervous tension. His story was a familiar one. Three months before he had lost his employment. His efficiency had steadily decreased until he believed himself unfit for work. On the very day of his visit he had an appointment with a man who was ready to offer him a lucrative position, but the youth lacked the courage to go through with the interview. The strain of repeated discouragements had manifested itself in domestic unhappiness. The young man summed up his experiences of the previous six months by declaring, "I've been living in Hell."

As we bowed our heads in prayer the whole story came out in broken sobs. The memory of a series of wrongdoings, committed five or six years before, had come back to plague him. They brought new sins in their wake. When the humiliating confession was over and he had sought and found the forgiveness of God he became a transformed man. The light of hope was in his eyes and confidence and courage in his heart. He kept his appointment with the man who had employment to offer him and secured a splendid position.

The Sunday following my interview with this young man he appeared at church with his attractive young wife. "We have enjoyed this week the greatest happiness we have ever known since our marriage," she confided to me. "Every night now at the close of the day we kneel together in prayer for God's blessing on our home."

That young man and his wife are now actively engaged in passing on to the boys and girls of a large Presbyterian Church the blessings that have come to them.

This type of ministry is one that is sorely needed at the heart of this great city, and some of you who listen to me will yet be my helpers in these glorious undertakings.

The message of St. James to the first-century Church is one that needs to be insistently proclaimed to men and women living in our own distressful times:

"Confess your faults one to another, and pray one for another, that ye may be healed. The effectual fervent prayer of a righteous man availeth much."

WHY MEN PLAY THE COWARD

And he said, I have been very jealous for the Lord God of hosts: for the children of Israel have forsaken thy covenant, thrown down thine altars, and slain thy prophets with the sword; and I, even I only, am left; and they seek my life, to take it away.

I KINGS 19:10

UNDOUBTEDLY one of the bravest men in all of Scotland's history was not a military or naval hero, but rather that dauntless preacher of righteousness, John Knox.

There had been gay festivities all night long in the palace of Mary, Queen of Scots. She and her court were rejoicing, for the news had come to them from across the Channel that there had been a widespread massacre of Protestants in France. Many hundreds had been killed. So Mary, the Catholic Queen, celebrated the event.

The next Sunday, in his morning sermon, John Knox denounced in unmeasured terms the rejoicings at the palace. He was fully aware that the Queen possessed the power of life and death over him, but he was quite unafraid.

Before many days had passed, he was summoned to

the palace to answer for his sermon. The servants of Mary, and the court minions, were deeply impressed by the fearless bearing of Knox in the presence of the Queen. As the preacher was leaving the audience chamber he heard one of the officers of the court declare, in amazement, "He is not afraid." Turning to the man, Knox said, "Why should the pleasing face of a gentlewoman affray me? I have looked into the faces of many angry men and have not been affrayed above measure."

The experience of Elijah recorded in the chapter from which our text is taken was different from that of Knox. A few days earlier he had taken his stand, on Mount Carmel, before all the multitude of Israel including eight hundred and fifty prophets of Baal. With a voice that rang through the mountain side, like a trumpet, he had declared: "How long go ye limping between the two sides? If the Lord be God, follow him, but if Baal, then follow him."

What a courageous man was Elijah! He towered like a colossus above the people of his day. He reminds us of Moses standing alone before Pharaoh; of John the Baptist denouncing Herod and Herodias; of Paul fearlessly proclaiming the judgment of the living God to Felix and Drusilla.

Not a week has passed since this scene was enacted on Carmel, but it seems to be a different Elijah who is pictured in our text. The man who could face a hostile multitude without flinching now flees in terror from the threats of a woman. The relentless Jezebel, bloodthirsty consort of Ahab, King of Israel, is on his trail. Her husband has told her of the destruction of the prophets of Baal and the news has filled her with wrath. She is made of sterner stuff than is Ahab. She is the Lady Macbeth of the Old Testament.

You will recall that dramatic scene in Shakespeare's play where the lord of the castle came down from the death chamber with the bloody daggers in his hands. He should have left them by the body of Scotland's King but, in his absent-mindedness and fear, he carried them away. He lacked the courage to go back again to the scene of the murder. Lady Macbeth snatched them from his trembling hands and cried: "Infirm of purpose, give me the daggers." A striking parallel might be drawn between the characters of Lady Macbeth and Jezebel on the one hand and Ahab and Macbeth on the other. The husband, in each case, was a willing partner in crime but lacked the cold-blooded resolution of his wife.

Jezebel swore a solemn oath and sent word of it to Elijah, saying: "So let the gods do to me, and more also, if I make not thy life as the life of these slain prophets of Baal by tomorrow at this time." She gave Elijah notice that he had just twenty-four hours to live, and she meant every word of it.

Who is this lone man fleeing away from the city of Beersheba to seek a hiding place in the wilderness? He is cowering in terror beneath a juniper tree. Now he is praying. Let us listen to his words: "It is enough. Now, O Lord, take away my life, for I am not better than my fathers."

That is the prayer of a beaten man. It is the whine of a defeated personality. It is the cry of a coward. Look at him closely. He wears a sheepskin mantle, with a leather girdle about his loins. Surely it cannot be Elijah! It is hardly possible that a man who withstood, singlehanded, eight hundred and fifty prophets of Baal could, in a few hours, sink into such dejection. But, in very truth, it is Elijah. The wrath of Jezebel has put him to rout.

The oath of the Queen reminds us of the forty young men who swore that they would neither eat nor drink until they had taken the life of the Apostle Paul. It reminds us also of the words of Richard, Duke of Gloucester, when he declared to his soldiers that he would not dine until Lord Hastings' head was brought to him.

Elijah's days were numbered, so it seemed. The unflinching Prophet has at last met defeat. It may sound strange to you, but I must say that I get a great deal of encouragement out of this incident. I am glad to discover that a man who was a mighty oak would sometimes bend before the storm.

Even the greatest of the prophets and saints have had their hours of weakness and depression. I hear Jeremiah saying: "The prophets prophesy falsely, and the people love to have it so." I hear Paul saying: "All they of Asia have turned from me, and only Luke is with me." Even Jesus, in an hour of bitter discouragement, when the multitude that had followed him began to melt away, turned to the little band of disciples beside him, and asked them sadly: "Will ye, also, go away?"

This lesson from the life of Elijah ought to help us, especially today, when so many people are meeting with reverses. There are those who have spent a lifetime saving some little competence against their old age, only to discover that, through unfortunate investments, their savings have crumbled away.

There are those who have put their lifeblood into the erection of a business structure, founded upon honesty and integrity, only to see it go to pieces before their eyes in the last five years.

There are those who have come upon a physical breakdown and who say in mournful tones, "There is nothing left now. When health is gone, everything is gone."

There are those who have been overwhelmed by personal sorrow and who say, "How heavy is my heart! How empty are my arms!"

Most pitiful of all are those who have met with shameful and humiliating moral defeat. Loathing and despising themselves the while, they weakly surrender with the coward's plea on their lips: "What's the use? I can't help it."

They are like Elijah under the juniper tree: "Now, O Lord, take away my life." There is no use going on. I am a beaten man.

The Prophet, in his conflict with the enemies of Jehovah, has had no opportunity either to rest or to eat and now, utterly overcome by physical exhaustion, he falls asleep.

With so many people today, like Elijah, seemingly at the end of their resources, we ought, surely, to be interested in what God did for him. And God did a surprising thing. His first prescription was not a spiritual remedy. It was rest and food. After the prophet had been refreshed by sleep the Angel of the Lord said to him: "Arise and eat."

Very often we overlook the fact that our physical

condition is frequently an important cause of spiritual depression. I have had people come to me with a religious problem and, after ministering to their pressing needs, have said to them, "Now go to a physician."

I am thinking of a youth who came back from the Great War cynical and embittered. He felt that life was hostile to him. It was not worth living. He constantly voiced his pessimistic philosophy. Fortunately, he had a wise and kindly father who said to him, "I shouldn't be worried, if I were you, about your present outlook. Wait a few months until you are built up physically, and then, I am sure, you will see life in brighter colors." Experience proved that the father was right.

One cannot blame many people today for being pessimistic and bitter. Oftentimes they lack two great necessities of life—sleep and food.

In the case of Elijah, we see the reaction that comes after a period of intense physical and mental activity. Sometimes a great orator who has played upon the emotions of a vast audience, as a virtuoso plays upon the keys of an organ, afterwards sinks into mental dejection.

How often have we seen a frail wife or mother keeping constant vigil, through weary months, beside the sickbed of a loved one until the crisis was passed for good or ill. Then came complete collapse.

So is it with Elijah. His words are those of a man who has lost his grip on life. The fight is out of him. He is whipped. He struggles on alone. He leaves his servant, who is a man of God, in Beersheba, while he journeys into the wilderness. Had he brought this companion with him he might have had a prayer meeting under that juniper tree.

For some reason or other, we desire to be alone when we are discouraged. Just when we need most of all the association of friends and loved ones, we go away by ourselves, until, in hopeless depression, we say: "O Lord, take away my life."

Have you noticed how frequently the first personal pronoun is used by Elijah? This is revealed especially in our text. "I have been very jealous for the Lord God of hosts: for the children of Israel have forsaken thy covenant, thrown down thine altars, and slain thy prophets with the sword; and I, even I only, am left; and they seek my life, to take it away." It is remarkable that a man so utterly devoid of fear as Elijah should now be trembling for the safety of his life. A few days before this, he would have said, "Well, what difference does it make? I was never so much in love with life that I should fear to lose it in the path of duty." But now he is a dispirited and broken man: "I, even I only, am left; and they seek my life, to take it away."

"Where now," he asks himself, "is the labor of men who have served God in days past—of Moses and Samuel, of David and Solomon? It has all gone for nothing, ending in the despotism of a Jezebel and in a nation that has turned its back upon God, an apostate people that have forsaken his covenants, thrown down his altars, slain his prophets with the sword."

There you have the outlook of a lonely, a dispirited, and a beaten man. What is the matter with

Elijah? He has forgotten the most important factor in the whole situation. He has forgotten God.

A few years ago, in Toronto, I had the privilege of a private conversation with Dr. Kagawa of Japan. We talked for more than an hour about the Kingdom of God. He said to me, "I have just come from the United States where I met with a group of ministers in a certain city. They reported on the religious situation there. Some of them said that the work of the Church was tremendously discouraging; that there was much popular indifference; that the forces of righteousness were plainly on the retreat. It was a very depressing meeting." After all the reports had been presented Dr. Kagawa was called upon. He said, "Brethren, haven't you left something out of your reckoning? Haven't you overlooked the most vital factor of all? You have forgotten God and his limitless power."

That was the trouble with Elijah. But suddenly as he cowers by the mouth of a cave in Mount Horeb, he hears the still small voice of the Eternal saying, "What doest thou here, Elijah? This is no place for my Prophet. It is true that Ahab has become apostate, and Jezebel, his wife, is seemingly triumphant, but go back, Elijah, and anoint a new king who will replace Ahab in Israel and anoint a new king over Syria."

Then the Prophet hears a final message which was the most surprising of all, "Go back, Elijah, and anoint your successor. Elisha, the son of Shaphat, must take up your work when you lay it down. And know that there are yet seven thousand in Israel who have not bowed the knee to Baal, and whose mouths have not kissed his image."

One can almost see the spirits of the Prophet rising and rising, until all sense of fear is driven out of his life. He goes back to face the bloody Jezebel and Ahab, King of Israel, to warn them that soon the judgment of God will fall upon their rebellious house.

What Elijah has experienced, when his physical needs were met, is a fresh realization of the presence and power of God. He is no longer alone. He would not dream, now, of saying: "I, I only, am left." Even if he should forget about the seven thousand faithful remaining in Israel, he would say, "I am not alone, for God is with me."

Human resources, without the undergirding of God, are but a broken reed. During one year of the depression, twenty-two thousand persons committed suicide in this country. So serious was the situation that the life-insurance companies were compelled to give special attention to this new element in the mortality rate. All these people had forgotten God. There is no such word as "failure" in the lexicon of a man who walks with him. One man with God is undefeatable.

A young woman came into my study in Winnipeg. She was poorly dressed and quite evidently discouraged. Her story was a sad though not an unfamiliar one. Her father was ill; her brothers unemployed. She was the sole wage earner in the home. Her health was failing. She was exceedingly nervous. Oftentimes she had lacked sufficient food.

"To crown it all," she said, "I fear that I shall lose my position, which is all that stands between my family and destitution. Even the employees in the office are talking about my appearance and I am constantly making mistakes in my work."

Her trembling hands and twitching lips revealed the fact that the case was critical. Before she left the church that young woman had found God. Her face was lighted up with new hope. Again and again she affirmed, "If God be for me, who can be against me?"

Twelve months later a young woman came to the church for an interview. She was simply but tastefully dressed. Her face was radiant. "Do you remember me?" she asked. I had to confess that I did not. Then with a quiet smile, she said, "If God be for me, who can be against me?" Instantly I recognized the one who had come to me in deep distress a year before. But the spirit of defeatism had vanished. She told me a thrilling story. Her unshakable faith in God had enabled her to triumph over every difficulty and had infused fresh courage into others in her home who had given up the battle. Like Elijah she had been lifted from despair and defeat into confident hope and victory.

May I say to the most depressed soul in this congregation, "No matter how hopeless the outlook may appear to be, a transformation will be wrought in you and in your circumstances when faith in God is rekindled in your heart; when you can declare with St. Paul, If God be for me, who can be against me? . . . I can do all things through Christ who strengtheneth me."

Do you not hear God speaking to you today? "What doest thou here, living in discouragement, in bitterness, with frustration dominating your life? This is the valley of defeatism and despair. Amid the rank fogs of pessimism is no place for a child of God to make his home." Rise up this morning, as Elijah did, in the strength of the Eternal and you will conquer splendidly at the very place where formerly you had failed.

ATHEISM, ITS CAUSE AND CURE

The fool hath said in his heart, There is no God.
PSALM 53:1

THERE is a Rabbinical tradition which records that directly above the couch of King David there always hung a harp. Sometimes at night the vagrant breezes, rippling over its strings, made such sweet music that the shepherd king would rise from his slumbers and match the strain with words, until dawn flecked with gold the eastern sky.

The prose of that poetic thought is this: that in the Psalms we have all the music of the heart of man as it is touched by the hand of God. "In it are gathered the lyrical burst of his tenderness, the moan of his penitence, the pathos of his sorrow, the triumph of his victory, the despair of his defeat, the firmness of his confidence, the rapture of his assured hope." As Dr. Heine says, "In it are collected sunrise and sunset, birth and death, promise and fulfillment—the whole drama of humanity." Here is the picture of man engaged in moral warfare, often defeated, sometimes driven to his knees, but always struggling to his feet again and pressing onward, realizing how short fulfillment falls of the goal which he has set before himself.

It is well for us to remember that the Psalm from which our text is taken was written about one thousand years before the birth of Christ, while we live in the twentieth century of the Christian era. It was written by a Hebrew, while we are mostly Anglo-Saxons. It was written by an Oriental king, while we are the subjects of a republic. Yet David, writing three millenniums ago, has penned a message which touches deeply the heart of each one of us. Every aspiration of the human spirit is expressed in the Psalter.

This Psalm blazes with indignation. The writer has met a man who declares that there is no God. He does not reason with the skeptic. He simply expresses his indignation and tells why no other conclusion could be expected of him.

You will search in vain through the Book of the Psalms for an argument for the existence of God. In all the teaching of Jesus not once does he debate this subject. Indeed, you will read through the Bible, from Genesis to Revelation, without finding any attempt to prove the existence of those spiritual truths in which every one of the saints and seers of the Bible believed. The reason is, of course, that God was so real, so personal, so definitely a fact of experience in the life of David, of Moses, of Isaiah, of Jesus, that they would as soon have thought of arguing about the reality of the resplendent sun as about the existence of God. They knew too well that the most precious experiences of life are not demonstrable in the sense that one would attempt to prove a proposition in Euclid. Tennyson's Ancient Sage has clearly expressed this:

Thou canst not prove the Nameless, O my son,
Nor canst thou prove the world thou movest in,

Thou canst not prove that thou art body alone,
Nor canst thou prove that thou art spirit alone,
Nor canst thou prove that thou art both in one.
Thou canst not prove thou art immortal, no,
Nor yet that thou art mortal—nay, my son,
Thou canst not prove that I, who speak with thee,
Am not thyself in converse with thyself,
For nothing worthy proving can be proven,
Nor yet disproven. Wherefore thou be wise,
Cleave ever to the sunnier side of doubt,
And cling to Faith beyond the forms of Faith!

The Bible writers and teachers knew full well that the most profound truths of religion can be apprehended only when they have been personally experienced. "The secret of the Lord is with them that fear him."

The same thought is expressed by F. W. H. Myers in his poem "St. Paul":

> O, could I tell, ye surely would believe it.
> O, could I only say what I have seen.
> How should I tell, or how can ye receive it?
> How, till he bringeth you where I have been?

"The fool hath said in his heart, There is no God." In this Psalm David declares that the denial of God is a belief which is born in the heart of a fool. But somebody objects to the language of our text, and says, "Isn't it unfair of David to use such a term to describe a man who doubts? Hasn't it oftentimes been said that the surest sign that one has lost out in an argument is the fact that he descends to abuse?

Is that not true of David, in the words of our text, when he calls an unbeliever a 'fool'?"

But the Psalmist is not descending to abuse. The word "fool" as it is used by David has quite a different content to the word as it is used in modern speech. The Hebrew word that the Psalmist wrote was "nābāl." It means not just a man who lacks sanity of judgment, but also a man who is ignoble, a blasphemer, an impious person, an immoral man. So we see that David is not employing abuse but is stating a fact. He has met a man who belongs to a class that has cast aside all moral restraint. From such a heart, says David, from the source or fountainhead of such a life one has no right to expect anything but a denial of God.

What David means by that word "fool" is made abundantly clear if you will read the remainder of the first verse of this Psalm: "The fool hath said in his heart, There is no God. Corrupt are they, and have done abominable iniquity: there is none that doeth good." You see, it is a special type of person the Psalmist is talking about, a type that can be fittingly described by that Hebrew word "fool."

In the first place, the Psalmist asserts that the denial of God in the lives of many people has its roots in a corrupt soil. "Every one of them is gone back," says David. "They are altogether become filthy; there is none that doeth good, no, not one." That approach to the problem of atheism lets in a flood of light upon it. It would be altogether unfair and untrue, of course, to suggest that all doubt springs from immoral living. The fact remains, however, that few people work out their philosophy of life and then pattern their lives according to it. It is usually the other way round. They choose the kind of life they desire to live and then frame their philosophy to justify their conduct.

When a man or woman comes to me with difficulties on the subject of the existence of God, I ask myself this question, "What kind of person is this? Do these outspoken doubts spring from a disordered life? Is this another case of the wish being father of the thought?" There are multitudes of people living in the modern world whose minds are clouded with doubt, not because of what they think, but because of what they are. They will have to make a clean break with their own past, before they can enter into a knowledge of God.

The huge lens just completed for the Mount Wilson telescope required years of careful preparation. The molten glass had to be poured with extraordinary care to avoid flaws or bubbles, otherwise it would have given a distorted view of the heavens. You cannot study the stars by looking through a telescope with marred lenses. Neither can any man hope to know, beyond all peradventure, the reality of God if he is looking through the eyes of a soul that is blemished and befouled with sin.

"Blessed are the pure in heart," said Jesus, "for they shall see God." Not in some far-distant heaven, but here and now will they have the vision of him.

Shortly after the close of the Great War, a friend of mine who is a Baptist minister in London, England, recounted an incident that illustrates exactly what I mean. If I recall it accurately, he had been a chaplain overseas. One day, in the course of his duties, he had visited a base hospital at Rouen in France. It was devoted to the care of soldiers who had enlisted to fight for their country but had been worsted in inner moral conflict and were paying the grievous penalty of their sins.

Said the chaplain, "As I was walking through one of the wards I suddenly noticed in a bed a young fellow who had been a Sunday-school teacher in my Church in London. I was glad to see that he was asleep and quickly slipped out of the ward, so that he would not know I had seen him there. The war dragged to an end and I went back to my pulpit in London. I waited to see that young man reappear in the church, but he didn't come. His Sunday-school class was without a teacher. After some months had passed, I was walking down the Strand when I met him face to face. I said, 'Tom, you haven't been in Sunday school lately. You have never come back to that class of boys you had. I haven't seen you in church once since you were discharged from the army. What's the matter?' "

"He looked up with a laugh, and said, 'Well, to tell you the truth, Padre, I have become a bit of a cosmopolitan. I don't believe the things that I used to accept. This talk about the Bible and Jesus is all right for Sunday-school children, but it doesn't go down with a grown-up man.' Then he added some words that bordered on blasphemy."

The chaplain looked him sternly in the eye, and said, "Tom, that's not the truth, and you know it. That's not where the trouble lies. I know what's the matter with you. It all goes back to that base hospital in Rouen, doesn't it, Tom?"

A flush of shame crept over the face of the young man, and, hanging his head, he said, "You are right, Padre, that is where the trouble is."

It was just one more case of a life's philosophy constructed to justify wrong conduct. There are tens of thousands of people like that. It was of them that the Psalmist was thinking when he said: "The fool, the impious and immoral man says in his heart, there is no God." And he finds relief in saying it.

In the second verse of this Psalm, the writer leads us into a deeper understanding of the problem. "God looked down from heaven upon the children of men, to see if there were any that did understand, that did seek God," says David. When God found men denying him, he looked to see if there were any who wanted to believe in him, who were seeking after him. Among that class, says the Psalmist, he found none. "Every one of them is gone back."

That explains a good deal for us even today. God looks down from Heaven to see if there are any that seek him. There are many that seek for money today and give their lives to that search. There are others who seek for personal advancement. And there are also those whose one aim in life seems to be the pursuit of pleasure. But none of them has even one minute to seek after God. Is it any wonder that God grows unreal to them; that spiritual things appear vague, shadowy, and insubstantial in contrast with material things? Yet these people who have not even a moment to give to the search for God are always ready to pass judgment upon the Christian Faith. "Be still, and know that I am God." How can we hope to know God in the precipitate rush of modern life?

I listened some years ago to an address by one of the officials of the National Gallery in London. He spoke of the way in which thousands of people visit that gallery. They come in with a rattle of heels on the pavement and a clatter of tongues, gallop through room after room with a hasty glance to the right hand and to the left, and then they talk of having "done" the National Gallery.

The lecturer said two yokels had come in from a country district in England, on their first visit to the capital city. They arrived at Trafalgar Square, and, while one man waited on the steps of the National Gallery to watch the traffic, the other went inside to see the paintings. After a little time, the second man came out. His comrade said, "Are you back so soon?" "Oh yes," said his friend. "I saw the whole thing in twenty minutes. If I had had my hobnail shoes on, I could have done it in fifteen."

That is not the way to read messages from the brush of great masters. Go to the Dutch Room in the National Gallery and see that Rembrandt painting of a Jewish rabbi. This work was done in the year 1657, a year after Rembrandt had become bankrupt. The background is a deep brown, and against that mellow glow is poised the rabbi's head. His dark hat casts a shadow over the upper part of his face. The light in the picture falls upon only one side, illuminating a little bit of his features not six inches square. All the rest is so dark as to be scarcely discernible.

On this small lighted surface, Rembrandt concentrates the full force of his genius. The weary eyes of the old man look out with ineffable sadness. The picture becomes, in a strange way, more than an individual portrait; it takes on a universal quality. Here we seem to have a glimpse of the sorrowing soul of humanity. We can each bring our own sorrows, and see them reflected there.

Study the sad light in those eyes, the wrinkles on that face, the indelible stamp of trouble printed there. You must be still to know Rembrandt.

"Be still, and know that I am God." "They that seek me shall find me," said the Lord. If God has become dim and unreal to you, if your mind is oftentimes clouded with doubt, ask yourself this question, "May it not be because I have failed to seek him or to give him a chance to find me?" If that be so, do not be surprised if some day a whisper will sound in your soul saying, "There is no God."

Finally, we read in the fourth verse that "they have not called upon God." Of course, that is true. Atheism is always prayerless. It cannot be otherwise. There is no fellowship with the Eternal: no meeting of Spirit with spirit, no experience of communion with the Divine when the soul is lifted up on wings of aspiration to visions of God. "They have not called upon God."

Invariably I ask of people who come to me to discuss these problems, "Have you ceased to pray?" That question is vital. For, just as surely as prayer ceases in your life, God will grow dim and unreal. You might as well imagine that the light in yonder bulbs could continue burning after the wires to the powerhouse had been cut as to think that knowledge of spiritual things can continue to abide in a life that has deliberately severed its one means of communication with God.

"Ask," says Jesus, "and ye shall receive; seek and ye shall find; knock and it shall be opened unto you." Make the experiment. Live on the assumption that God exists and seek to commune with him. He will respond to your search. Your quest is ended when you are truly willing to be found of him.

Some years ago I had the privilege of traveling with Dr. F. B. Meyer of Christ Church, London. In his own quiet way he talked to me of all that faith in God had meant to him. In his prayers he communed with God as though the Eternal were in the room beside him. I said to him one day during the journey, "Dr. Meyer, I hope you will pardon the question, but are there never any hours when your faith in God grows dim, when doubt clouds your vision?" He turned to me with his kindly smile and answered, "I am glad you asked me that. It is nearly seventy years now since I gave my heart to God. I am getting old and frail now and I depend on him for everything. In all those seventy years he has never failed me once. Not even for a moment does the vision grow dim." I can still see the dear old man, his face radiant with the light of Heaven, as he made his wonderful confession. A year or two after that God called him Home.

This is the one pathway in life that becomes more radiant as the years roll by, for upon it glows the light that shineth more and more unto the perfect day. Without Him the road is bleak and lonely. The unbelief that ends in the denial of God saps ideals, quenches hope, paralyzes every effort for human betterment and enthrones despair in the heart. He who walks with God is not promised immunity from the trials and tribulations of life, but he is given strength and courage with which to overcome the world.

The Eternal God is with us. Let us then adventure forth this morning with erect heads and brave hearts to live triumphantly and to "greet the unseen with a cheer."

THREE CROSSES ON A HILL CREST

I. The Impenitent Thief

And one of the malefactors which were hanged railed on him, saying, If thou be Christ, save thyself and us.

LUKE 23:39

IN THE New Testament there are four accounts of the trial, crucifixion, and death of Jesus. Each of the Evangelists adds something to our knowledge of that awful tragedy. The four gospels have one notable characteristic in common: they all record, with an amazing detachment, our Lord's suffering and death.

How can this be? Unquestionably, we have a description by eye-witnesses of these scenes. These men loved Jesus with passionate intensity. They were heartbroken at his death. They recognized the injustice of all that had overtaken him. Yet, as they describe the successive outrages—the mocking and scourging he was compelled to undergo, the procession to Calvary, and the long-drawn-out agony and death when his pain-wracked soul at last found peace—they record it all in dispassionate words. It would have been easy for them to have emphasized the tortures that were inflicted upon their Master, to have described at length the horrors of his death, to have hurled burning words of condemnation at Pilate and Herod, at Caiaphas and the Jewish mob; but there is none of this in the record of the Evangelists. They simply record what transpired, and let the facts speak for themselves.

In the unprejudiced history of the happenings on that black day, there is scarcely anything more impressive than the words that tell of the attitude of the soldiers in front of the cross: "And sitting down, they watched him there." Indeed, it is this impartial attitude on the part of the Gospel writers that impresses us with the reality and truthfulness of the record.

Anyone who has read a description of a crucifixion, in the writings of the Ancients, must be impressed with the accuracy, even to the smallest detail, of the accounts that have been given to us by the Evangelists.

It was a Roman Governor who pronounced the death sentence upon Jesus. Crucifixion did not originate with the Romans. They borrowed the practice from their enemies, the Carthaginians. It was a death reserved for slaves, seditionists, and criminals of the lowest class. The Romans always preceded a crucifixion by scourging. So terrible was this punishment that the victim often died under the lash and was spared the later indignities of the cross. After the scourging the criminal was made to carry his cross to the place of execution. There he was stripped naked and nailed or bound to the cross, as it lay on the ground, or after it had been set up into position. The victim was then left to die of exhaustion, thirst, or wounds. Sometimes he lingered for as long as two whole days.

It was the practice of the Romans to resort to the crurifragium to end the lingering agony of the condemned. Soldiers broke the bones of the dying men with iron hammers, thus hastening the end by shock.

When judgment had been pronounced upon a prisoner, the Roman magistrate caused the crime of which he had been convicted to be recorded, in black letters, on a board coated with white gypsum. Pilate, the Roman Governor, mortified by the fact that the Jewish leaders had forced his hand in the case of Jesus, secured at least a partial revenge by writing on this board that Jesus was "the King of the Jews." To the protest of Caiaphas and the other leaders, that he should have recorded this merely as a claim on the part of Jesus, Pilate replied contemptuously, "What I have written I have written." This notice was fastened to the top of the cross above the head of the Nazarene.

How little can we, who live in the twentieth century and in a Christian land, realize the awfulness of the death that Jesus suffered! We sing "In the Cross of Christ I glory." We build churches in the form of a cross. We put crosses on altars and on church spires. We even carry the cross as a watch charm or as a personal adornment. But how little we know of the experience of crucifixion!

Those who have been in the city of Antwerp in Belgium and have seen Rubens' masterpiece, "Christ between Two Thieves," have caught at least a glimpse of the horrible reality. Here is what one critic says about that painting: "Struggle is the word that describes this picture. It is an embodiment of physical agony, unillumined by a single ray of spiritual meaning." That is true. The painting is remarkable for the fact that it is almost devoid of religious feeling. It exhibits only the agony, the tension, the torture to which the three victims were subjected. Christ is represented as already dead, but there is no relaxation in his muscles. He seems to be suffering still. One of the thieves has struggled until he has torn one foot free from the restraining spike. Both brigands are writhing on their crosses. A soldier is climbing, by means of a ladder on the nearest cross, and with his crurifragium is about to break the legs of one of the victims. Longinus, about whom so many legends have clustered, is piercing the side of Christ with a spear. It is a horrible picture, almost revolting in its realism, as it portrays the utter brutality of the human heart. How strange that he who lived only to bless and to help men should have been compelled to die between two thieves. The words of the Prophet Isaiah have at last reached fulfillment: "He was numbered with the transgressors and he bare the sin of many."

Who were these men destined to die with our Lord? No doubt they had commenced their rebellious careers as zealots. They were eager to overthrow the rule of Rome. But insurrection was a dangerous business and Rome was remorseless in her punishment of offenders. The Jew who lifted up his hand against the Empire was marked for death. He had to creep through the lanes and back streets of the cities, or live as an outlaw amid mountain fastnesses. It was a hardening and brutalizing experience. Many of these men who had commenced their career with a noble resolve to free their country from a hated oppressor ended up as common robbers and murderers.

The parable that Jesus told of the man who was waylaid, robbed, and beaten almost to death, on the road from Jericho to Jerusalem, was an illustration drawn from an oft-repeated incident of his time.

Rome had laid her heavy hand upon these two thieves. They had been captured by her soldiers. They were brought before Pontius Pilate and sentenced to death by crucifixion. It is quite probable that sentence was passed upon them the day before Jesus was tried by the Roman Governor.

When our Lord started on the journey to Golgotha, beside him were two thieves dragging their crosses. They were coarse, hardened, savage men. They poured forth their scorn upon the Roman soldiers in fierce and blasphemous oaths.

From an account of a crucifixion, given by Cicero, the Roman orator and statesman, we learn that it was usual for the victim of that horrible fate, frenzied with pain, to shriek, entreat, curse, and spit at the spectators gathered around the cross. We may be sure that the Jewish outlaws who died on Calvary vented, to the limit of their strength, their hate and contempt upon the soldiers and the mob.

Suddenly both these criminals realized that no word of reproach had fallen from the lips of the man on the central cross. As they looked at his face, wan with suffering but full of tenderness, they saw that his eyes were closed in prayer. Then they heard the most wonderful words that ever fell upon human ears: "Father, forgive them, for they know not what they do." That compassionate entreaty dropped right into the heart of one of those hardened men, and "chords that had long been broken began to vibrate once again."

But the other thief remained wholly untouched. "If thou be the Christ," he cried, revealing by his words a knowledge of Jewish faith, "if thou be the Messiah, save thyself and us." The outlaw would recognize the unique claims of Jesus if he will but save himself. But that was the one thing that Jesus could not do. Love would not let him. Because he was the Messiah, the Christ, God's Chosen One, he could not save himself. The Jewish leaders little realized how truthfully they spoke when they taunted the suffering Man on the cross with the words: "He saved others, himself he cannot save." It is in the very nature of self-sacrifice that he who saves others cannot save himself.

During the Spanish-American War yellow fever killed many thousands more American soldiers than all the bullets of the Spaniards. In Cuba, during the year 1900, one-third of the officers of General Leonard Wood's staff died of this dread disease. Havana was overrun with it. The American Government sent out Major Walter Reed, a medical officer, to see what could be done in combating this scourge. He had two chief assistants, Drs. James Carroll and Jesse Lazear.

A certain type of mosquito was believed to be the carrier of the bacteria, but this had not been proved. Dr. Reed and his assistants must establish this fact beyond all doubt. As they walked through the military hospitals and looked into the faces of these doomed American boys, delirious, with bloodshot eyes and faces yellow as the leaves of Autumn, dying like flies, they set themselves resolutely to their task. It was necessary that healthy men be bitten by mosquitoes that had fed on the blood of yellow-fever victims. But who was prepared to make that sacrifice? The investigators themselves volunteered.

On September the thirteenth Jesse Lazear was sitting at the bedside of a victim who was tossing with the fever when a mosquito that had been feeding on many of the patients in the ward lit upon his hand. Calmly he watched the creature feel around with her stinger and then dig it in as she drank her fill and swelled up into a bright balloon with his blood. He knew the risk he was taking, but the plague must be stamped out and human lives saved.

Five days later Lazear was in bed with headache and fever. Quickly his temperature mounted to one hundred and four degrees, his pulse to one hundred and six. In less than a week this entry was made in the records of the hospital: "The death of our lamented colleague, Jesse Lazear, aged 34 years, occurred on the eve of September 25, 1900." He had perished a martyr to science but by his death he had saved countless thousands of lives. He saved others, himself he could not save.

"If thou be the Christ, save thyself." "Come down from the cross." But that, Christ cannot do. It is not the nails which hold him there. It is redeeming love. "He saved others, himself he cannot save."

It was purely a selfish motive that prompted the cry of the impenitent thief. He was thinking of his own safety. He says: "Save thyself and us." The depravity of the man's heart is revealed by his request.

"This thief utters no cry for pardon; has no sense of the exceeding sinfulness of sin; no dream of a better life rises within his mind; no remorse because of his misspent hours and talents seems to move him. . . . He is the same foul-mouthed and murderous brigand, only crucified and impotent." He hates Jesus because of his tenderness and patience. He desires only escape from the fierce punishment that has been visited upon him. He has no wish to be freed from his sins. He wants to return to them. He desires only escape from pain.

The tragedy of the unrepentant human heart has often been borne in upon me as I have preached to convicts in Canadian penitentiaries. I have had scores of interviews with these men. I have seen hardened hearts completely broken with contrition. I have watched souls being born again. But every now and then, into the interview room would come a man apparently in deep distress, and I would say, "What can I do for you, my friend?" The answer would be, "Will you please write to the Minister of Justice to see if I can get a parole?" There was no sorrow for the past, no realization of the justice of his punishment, no desire for reform; only a longing to escape the penalty of wrongdoing.

There is no need to go to penitentiaries to find people like that. There are thousands of them in every city of this land, sinners who love their sin and desire to escape only from the suffering that it brings.

What was the response of Jesus? He had nothing whatsoever to say. He made no answer, simply because there was nothing more to be said. To my mind, that is one of the most solemnizing incidents recorded in the Bible. It is a terrible fact of human experience that there can come a time in the life of a man when God has nothing more to say to him. Jesus had talked with Caiaphas. He had reasoned with Pilate. He had grieved over Judas. He had prayed for Peter. But to the impenitent thief he had not a word to say. The capacity for spiritual reformation had died within the outlaw's heart. "Ephraim is joined to his idols; let him alone."

Dante in his *Divine Comedy* tells of his journey into the unseen world. He was guided to those spirits who, up to the last moment of their lives, had been sinners, but heeding at length the warning of Heaven had repented and were forgiven. In the poet's words, they "did issue out of life at peace with God." Among them, Dante is surprised to see one Buonconte who on earth had been sensuous, rebellious, and vile. How came he to be among those who journey on to the vision of God? Buonconte answers that, stricken in battle, he had fled away, leaving on the plain a gory trail from a gaping wound in his throat. As he lay dying, the minions of Hell came swooping down to bear him away, but swifter than thought God's angels had also come and stood on guard. They debated for possession of his soul. So black was Buonconte's record that he believed himself forever lost. But just as the demons were claiming him for their own, an angel pointed to his eyelids, weighed down in the last long sleep, where, hanging from their fringe, was "one poor tear." It was the token of repentance. At the last moment he had turned his face to God. Triumphantly the angels bore him to the Realms of the Redeemed.

But when, amid the darkness and horror of Calvary, the last convulsive throb of agony had shaken the mighty frame of the impenitent thief, on his eyelids, forever closed in death, there was not even "one poor tear." He died, as he had lived, in rebellion against God and man. Within one arm's length of salvation, with the Savior of the world so near to him that he could almost touch his hand, he turned his face to the outer darkness where the worm dieth not and the fires of remorse are not quenched. May God, in His mercy, preserve us all from the sin of impenitence!

THREE CROSSES ON A HILL CREST

II. The Penitent Thief

And he said unto Jesus, Lord, remember me when thou comest into thy kingdom.

And Jesus said unto him, Verily I say unto thee, to-day shalt thou be with me in paradise.

LUKE 23:42, 43

NO EVENT in human history has so arrested the attention of mankind as the crucifixion of Jesus Christ. The eyes of all generations have been drawn to his cross. Tens of thousands of books have been written upon this theme. More than fifty master-painters, including the greatest names in the realm of art, have chosen it as a subject upon which to lavish their genius. Yet the tragedy of Golgotha remains wrapped in mystery as deep and impenetrable as the darkness that shrouded Calvary on the evening of our Lord's death. But the love and compassion that ever radiates from the face of the Crucified One has continued to bring healing and forgiveness to many a broken and contrite heart.

While the multitude on the mountain side watched, with bated breath, the successive stages of the brutal crime which sinful human passions had made inevitable, another drama was enacted which only those about the cross could see. The love of God in Christ was striving to win the souls of the two thieves who hung beside our Lord. What a subject this would make for the brush of some great master! On one cross impenitence; on the other penitence, and in the midst Redeeming Love. The face of one thief is twisted with a sneer of contempt and hate, and the features of the other lighted up with the dawning peace of God.

It is altogether likely that these men were comrades in crime. Pontius Pilate, the Roman Governor, had found them guilty of robbery, and perhaps also of murder. They were fierce, cruel, brutalized men. Oftentimes they had lain in wait for some unsuspecting traveler on the highways of Judea or Galilee. Having robbed and slain their victim, they divided the spoils. Their perilous life had made them friends. They shared common dangers and adventures. All men were regarded by them as legitimate prey. They had nothing but contempt for justice and righteousness.

When, at last, these robbers fell into the hands of Roman soldiers, and heard the sentence that condemned them to unspeakable torture on the cross, they both resolved that they would not gratify their captors by the slightest evidence of weakness. On the central cross they saw the third victim of Rome's vengeance. His gentleness called forth their scorn. Instinctively they realized that this was a righteous man. So they joined with the mob, as two of the Evangelists make quite plain, in hurling taunts and jeers on his defenseless head.

Suddenly something arrests the attention of one of the thieves. He has been watching Jesus. From the crowd around the cross he has heard scraps of gossip, which reveal to him that here is no ordinary man. This hardened outlaw is convinced that Jesus is innocent of any crime. His is not the face of a criminal. In spite of all the words of mockery that are directed at him, there is no resentment in his eyes. No word of protest or defense falls from his lips. Only love and compassion are reflected on his face. Just as the thief is on the point of shouting some term of contempt at our Lord, he stops. The words are frozen on his lips. He sees that the Master's eyes are closed in prayer. From a heart torn with grief and pain there comes the cry: "Father, forgive them, for they know not what they do."

Luke is the only Evangelist who records this prayer of Jesus. He alone tells of the conversion of the thief.

I believe there is a definite relationship between the words of our Lord and the transformation wrought in the life of the outlaw who heard them. Is it too much to ask you to believe that a prayer of ten words could break a heart that was as hard as flint, could open a way to Heaven from the very gates of Hell?

Never have I been able to read Luke's story of the penitent thief without thinking of Tokichi Ishii, who, a little more than fifteen years ago, waited in a Tokio prison for the hour of his execution. He had been convicted of highway robbery, burglary, prison-breaking, and of five separate murders.

Ishii was forty-seven years of age, and half of his

life had been spent in prison. He was uneducated, steeped in crime, and one of the most feared of Japanese outlaws.

As he sat in his little cell waiting for the hour of death, two missionaries passed by and handed him a New Testament. He placed it, unopened, on a shelf. One day when he had nothing else to do, he took it down and began to read, in his own language, the story of the crucifixion of Christ. He became interested. Here was a man who, though he was innocent, was condemned and unjustly put to death. Apparently he was kind and good. His life was devoted to leading men into paths of virtue. To Tokichi Ishii, criminal though he was, it seemed an inhuman thing so to torture a noble and guiltless man.

As the condemned murderer continued to read the story in the Gospel of Luke, his attention was suddenly arrested by these words: "Then said Jesus, Father, forgive them, for they know not what they do." It seemed unbelievable to Ishii that, at the very moment when Jesus' life was being taken from him, he should pray for his murderers. Ishii says: "I stopped. I was pierced as by a five-inch nail."

In his narrow cell the hardened criminal at that moment came face to face with Jesus Christ and was lifted up and redeemed. He became as gentle as a child. The story of his conversion went throughout the length and breadth of the country. He made no effort to seek a reprieve. On the morning of August 18, 1918, Ishii walked to his death with a radiant light on his face, and the peace of God in his heart. His last words were in the form of a poem:

My name is defiled,
My body dies in prison;
But my soul purified
To-day returns to the City of God.

If the prayer of Jesus for the forgiveness of his enemies, when read in the New Testament nineteen centuries after the crucifixion, could transform the life of Japan's greatest criminal, what must have been the effect of those words on the penitent thief as he heard them falling fresh from the lips of our Lord? So near to Jesus was this man that he could see the lines of anguish on the Master's face and trace the rivulets made by the blood drops that flowed down from the thorns encircling his brow. In a moment of time the whole life of this brigand passed before his eyes. He saw the futility, the shame, and the failure of it all. The prayer of Jesus broke his heart.

You recall how Browning in *The Ring and the Book* tells of a certain night at Naples. So dark was it, he says, that one could scarce have guessed that anywhere about was earth, or sky, or sea, or world at all.

> But the night's black was burst through by a blaze.

One flash of lightning revealed the surrounding mountains, the city thick with spires, and the sea white like a ghost. "So," says the poet, "truth may be flashed out by one blow," and in that instant the despairing soul may see and be saved. Thus it was with the thief on the cross. Only a few minutes before, this man had joined his voice to the curses and imprecations that were heaped upon Jesus. But now, overwhelmed with penitence, he implores God's mercy on his sinful life. "Therefore, if any man be in Christ he is a new creature. Old things are passed away. Behold, all things are become new."

The genuineness of the conversion that has overtaken the penitent thief is revealed by his changed attitude to Jesus. He who had sided with the enemies of our Lord now boldly becomes his defender. Addressing his companion in crime, he says: "Dost not thou fear God, seeing thou art in the same condemnation? And we indeed justly; for we receive the due reward of our deeds: but this man hath done nothing amiss."

True repentance is ever revealed in assent to the justice of the punishment that sin brings on itself. One thief had cried: "If thou be Christ save thyself and us." He wished to escape the penalty of sin; but the other declares: "We receive the due reward of our deeds." Turning his face to Jesus, he said: "Lord, remember me when thou comest into thy kingdom." He does not ask that he may be saved from the cross. He does not request release from suffering. He accepts the torture without complaint. Indeed, he would not have one pang less. "He bares his breast, as it were, to the knife, and pleads that there be no sparing of pain."

His past life, marred and stained with sin, is now crucified on that cross. The billows of agony that surge over him are like cleansing streams that wash away his defilement. He is being born again.

How the Master must have exulted with joy when he heard a plea for pardon on the lips of the repentant thief! He had made no protest against the indignities of the Roman soldiers; he seemed not to hear the jeering of the mob; he remained silent to the selfish plea of the impenitent thief; but now, he who had been deaf to all this responds at once to a cry of contrition and, with a look of surpassing tenderness, says to the awakened soul beside him: "Verily, I say unto thee, to-day shalt thou be with me in paradise."

The two thieves are separated by only a few feet and yet they

are leagues apart on their crosses, not by the measurement of space but by the measurement of the spirit. They have been united in an unholy brotherhood in the bonds of theft and violence, but that union has been forever broken. The one spends his last breath in blasphemous reviling, and the other in a prayer for forgiveness. One goes down to death with the marks of shame and infamy upon him, and the other is snatched like a brand from the burning.

Does not all this point us to the only true solution for one of the most baffling problems in the life of this nation? I refer to the problem of crime. Up to the present, we have largely tried to solve it by force: by building stronger penitentiaries, by increasing the penalty for lawbreakers, by making crime detection more efficient. Unquestionably, all these methods have had their value and produced results. But no sooner has one gang been exterminated than another takes its place. We are breeding criminals so fast that the forces of law and order cannot cope with them.

There are those who tell us now that the remedy will be found in a totally different direction. They assure us that we must transform the conditions under which many people live by providing better housing in slum areas, opportunities for healthful recreation, and an environment in which boys and girls may live their lives untainted by the influences of crime. There is not the slightest doubt that such methods will do much to eliminate the soil in which wrong-doing flourishes. But if we stop there, we shall have failed again. It is not enough to change the environment while leaving men themselves unchanged. Important as are all these methods, they are secondary to the influence of religion. The growth of crime has kept pace with the decay of religion in the home. The greatest criminals of our day come from a home environment where neither God nor man is feared.

Society has tried education, repression, kindness, and punishment, but it has not succeeded in making bad men good, thieving men honest, foul men clean. But what society has failed to do, the Gospel of Christ can achieve. A resurgence of true religion in the life of this nation, penetrating into the homes and lives of our people, would do more to solve the problem of crime than all the laws that Congress can enact.

As I penned this sermon, there came back to me the recollection of a preaching mission which I held a little over a year ago in a penitentiary in Western Canada. The Spirit of God was mightily manifest in that institution. At the close of each service many convicts came to me for personal interviews. Among them was a veritable giant of a man, towering six feet, five inches, in height. He was even then a serious problem to the penitentiary staff. He had been a rum runner, bank robber, and was serving a fifteen-year sentence for "robbery with violence." For years he had been estranged from his wife and children. Just as he had won the penitent thief, Christ laid his hand upon that man and made him a new creature. On his knees, in the presence of God, he confessed his sins and found forgiveness and peace. Shortly afterwards he was reconciled to his wife and children.

When I was leaving the penitentiary, he gave me a letter to his wife and said, "You can make whatever use of this letter you please." According to prison regulations, of course, it was open. I quote from it one paragraph, which I copied. Speaking of his interview with me, he wrote:

> In his presence I made the first prayer to God that ever left my lips, and now I am able to hold my head up again before any human being, regardless of my past sins. I was always unhappy before that prayer, but I feel happy now because that prayer was for you and the children. God, how I have thought about them! There has never been a night that I have not imagined their little arms around my neck saying: "Nite, nite, daddy." Oh! What a fool a man can become. I started with a minor sin, and how they can grow into big ones without one realizing their growing! . . . But now, although I am inside grey walls, I am a free man.

That convict is secretary of a Bible class of forty prisoners, which meets every week in a Manitoba penitentiary.

Just before I left Winnipeg last summer, the warden said to me, "This prisoner is worth more to me than any three guards I have in the institution. He keeps everybody in good humor with his wonderful spirit. One never need fear trouble while he is around. Some day, when his sentence has expired, he will be a useful member of society."

John Masefield, Britain's poet laureate, in his poem "The Everlasting Mercy" tells of a woman who went down, step by step, the pathway of degradation and shame, until, at last, in despair she was tempted to get

> The river's help to mend the life
> Too wrecked for man to mend.

What tragedy is encompassed by these words, "Too wrecked for man to mend." That was true of the thief on the cross; of my friend in the penitentiary; of thousands of others beaten in life's conflict. Man is powerless to reclaim, re-create, restore. But the glory of the gospel which I proclaim to the most discouraged soul here today is that no life is "too wrecked for Christ to mend."

It is growing dark on Calvary. You can scarcely see the Cross stark against the sky. What is the meaning of that awful cry? Let us draw near. The taunts and jeers are hushed. There is no use reviling the Galilean; he no longer hears. His head has fallen forward on his breast. He is dead. But the thieves are both alive. Sturdy fellows these to suffer so long. Here come the Roman soldiers with the crurifragium to break their bones.

Look at that dying thief! His eyes are fixed on the face of Christ. He does not see the soldiers. He does not seem to know that death is near. What sickening blows those Romans strike! He is almost gone. What is that the man is saying? "Today . . . in paradise . . . with him."

THREE CROSSES ON A HILL CREST

III. The Christ between the Thieves

And with him they crucify two thieves, the one on his right hand, and the other on his left.

MARK 15:27

ONE does not hear many sermons in our time on the subject of the Cross of Christ. That theme has lost its central place in modern preaching. We hear of Christ as an example, a leader, a guide, a martyr, a hero of faith; but only seldom as Savior and Redeemer.

Few, indeed, are the preachers who could say to their congregation what St. Paul wrote to the Church at Corinth: "I determined not to know anything among you save Jesus Christ and him crucified." In the preaching of the Apostolic Church this sublime subject was unceasingly proclaimed. Christ was always lifted up. Tens of thousands of sermons are delivered every Sunday on this Continent, yet these messages seem to lack the transforming power that once lent itself to the preaching of the Word. May not this spiritual sterility be explained, at least in part, by the fact that the central theme of Christian faith has all too often been relegated to the circumference?

Why has the Cross lost the place of preeminence in Christian preaching that once it held? The main reason, I think, is that it has been obscured in the minds of ministers by the multitude of contemporary problems that cry out for a solution.

We are living in a day when the hearts of men and women are failing them for fear. We are driven almost to distraction by our anxieties. Over the whole earth hang the black clouds of impending war. Unemployment is rampant everywhere, bringing hunger, wretchedness, and misery in its wake. Crime continues to exact a dreadful toll of society. Race hatred is poisoning the springs of human relations. The fires of persecution are blazing again. The world is in a desperate situation. Many a preacher will say, "We dare not refrain from dealing with these issues that are uppermost in the minds and hearts of the men and women who listen to us week by week. They are looking to us for guidance and direction. We must not fail them. It is irrelevant to dwell upon a Cross that was uplifted nineteen centuries ago when, in the world around us, thousands are being crucified upon the cross of want and persecution."

What shall we reply to this contention? How shall we answer the insistent protest that our present problems, which are so grave and pressing as to threaten the existence of civilization, should concern us more vitally than the tragedy of Golgotha many centuries ago ?

The answer was given to me in a manner never to be forgotten when I traveled in Europe some eighteen months ago. In company of a group of American citizens I visited ten countries there. We were in Germany immediately after Hitler's blood purge and witnessed its terrible aftermath. We visited, in Russia, scores of dismantled churches turned into anti-religious museums. We arrived in Austria while Vienna was still in a ferment over the murder of Dollfuss. For weeks we lived on a continent torn by dissension, hate, fear, greed, persecution and dwelling under the overshadowing menace of war. Near the close of that eventful summer we journeyed to the little town of Oberammergau in the Bavarian Alps. At once we seemed to be in a different world. It was remote from all the strife and tension which had been our lot. Scarcely an echo of the turmoil reached us there.

Then one day for almost six hours we watched the players portraying the Passion of our Lord. As we beheld the characters in the drama filling their appointed rôles, each playing his part in the tragic climax that sent Christ to the Cross, suddenly it dawned upon us that we were witnessing on that stage the same hateful passions holding sway that were filling Europe with disorder and threatening the peace and safety of the whole world. In the Cross of Calvary we had found an explanation of the malady from which mankind is suffering and which has brought the world to its present state of distress. The selfsame sins that made inevitable the death of Jesus are as active in the world around us—yea, in your life and in mine—as when they sent the Son of Man to his undeserved doom. Evil is one vast, corporate force throughout the ages. The selfishness and greed, the lust and hate revealed on Calvary are identical with the evil impulses which we cherish in our hearts.

"The spark of electricity which meets the touch of one's hand on a metal knob of a winter's morning is one with the bolt of lightning which wrecks a house."

That is the reason why men and women, as they have looked upon the Cross, have felt themselves involved in that tragedy as though they actually had played a part in the crucifixion of our Lord. Indeed, when we think of the Cross as an eternal experience in the heart of God, there is a sense in which this is literally true. For have we not all at some time or other allowed those selfsame sins to have dominion over us which made inevitable his death?

Look at the sins that crucified Christ! Peter denied him because he was put to rout by a woman's scorn. Have you and I never denied our Lord, to escape the scoffing of his enemies? Judas betrayed Jesus for thirty pieces of silver. Have we never betrayed him, when by setting aside his commandments we insured for ourselves material gain?

Pilate condemned Jesus because his position as Roman Governor was of more concern to him than the life of an innocent Galilean. Have we never been guilty of securing our comfort, our position, our safety at the expense of the welfare of others?

Caiaphas rejoiced in the death of Jesus because at last it gave him an opportunity to vent to the full his prejudices and hate. Have we never wounded the heart of fellow creatures by our bias and our resentments?

The Roman soldiers keeping guard on Golgotha passed the time gambling with dice while our Lord writhed in anguish on the Cross! Are there none today, even among professing Christians, who as lightly pass the time in vapid pleasures, callously indifferent to the needs and sufferings of those around them?

"Were you there when they crucified my Lord?" asks the plaintive spiritual! If the truth be known we were all there and we were not standing with his friends.

The Cross of Christ not relevant to the problems of today! God pity our blindness. It's the only theme that truly ministers to contemporary human needs.

When one looks out over this nation and observes its political and social, its business and industrial life he is compelled to admit that nothing short of a revolution in the present outlook of men and women—a complete change of heart—will ever make possible the abolition of injustice and greed and the coming of God's Kingdom in this land. And what can change the hearts of men? Will education do it? Will legislation? Will coercion? We have tried all these means and they have largely failed. One thing yet remains—the Gospel of Jesus Christ. We must preach that message with renewed conviction and rekindled passion, lifting high the Cross of Christ as a redemptive and transforming power in the lives of men and women, until, as of old, he will draw all men unto him.

Not only does the Cross reveal the collective sins of the race in all their repulsiveness but it enables us to see the sin of individual men and women as it appears to the eyes of God.

The sense of sin is not vital today. We are often reminded that people are not worrying about their sins in our time. Several schools of thought have assured us that there is no occasion to worry about sin; that it is nonexistent.

There are those who argue from mistaken implications of the theory of evolution. They contend that sin for man is inevitable and inescapable. They represent it as the remains of our brute ancestry; an unavoidable inheritance of animal appetites and impulses.

There are religious cults, too, who join in assuring us that sin has no reality. It is "a mistake of mortal mind." It is "the shadow where the light ought to be." It is "a discord that has been struck where harmony should reign."

Then, too, there are the moral sophisticates like Mrs. Bertrand Russell, who solemnly asserts that "the idea of sin must be banished" in order that people may be truly happy. If she had told us how sin itself could be banished she might have made a real contribution to human happiness.

Oscar Wilde declares that "sin, with its curiosities, widens the horizons of life. Prejudices and prohibitions are mere walls to imprison the soul."

These are but two voices from a vast chorus which assures the present generation that ideas of sin are old fashioned and out of date. It is true that there is no vital sense of sin in the modern mind and one of the reasons for this, I believe, is the fact that the Church all too frequently has ceased to hold aloft the Cross of Jesus Christ.

Sin comes to us today in the form of attractive personalities. It is dressed up in bright colors. It is alluring. It gives promise of happiness and pleasure. But when we stand before the Cross we see sin with all the glamour and tinsel stripped away—a stark, hellish, ugly thing. Under the shadow of Calvary it is shown up in its true colors and its unspeakable shame as "a blow struck in the face of God's Holy Love."

Even William Lecky, the rationalist and philosopher, speaks of Jesus as "that ideal character which, through all the changes of eighteen centuries, has filled the hearts of men with impassioned love." How could it be otherwise? He never once thought of himself. He spent his strength in the service of the poor, the sick, the outcasts, the oppressed, the sinful; healing, teaching, uplifting, redeeming. He sought no reward save the joy of helping others. He came to reveal God to man and to lift men up to God. And yet him men have taken "and by wicked hands have crucified and slain."

In the Cross of Christ we see unveiled the exceeding sinfulness of sin and the depravity of the human heart. No such thing as sin! Tens of thousands of broken hearts and despairing lives testify to its devastating power. No such thing as sin! Tell that to the young wife, whom I know, who is sobbing away her days overwhelmed by the disgrace of a husband's sin; and who bears in her own body its awful scars. Her only fault was that she trusted too much. No such thing as sin! Tell that to the brokenhearted father, whose gray hairs are being brought down with sorrow to the grave. He has seen an honored name dragged through the mire by a worthless son, who must spend the best years of his life behind prison bars. No such thing as sin! Tell that to the young man, whom I know in New York, who, only a few weeks ago, jested about sin but who today sits with his face in his hands, overwhelmed with remorse, while the dearest hopes of life lie in fragments at his feet. Sin, which has wrought these tragedies, is laid bare in the Cross of Christ.

Again, not only does the Cross reveal the collective and individual sins of the race, but it is also the place where deliverance is found.

John Bunyan, in his *Pilgrim's Progress,* says: "Just as Christian came up with the cross, his burden loosed from off his shoulder and fell from off his back and began to tumble and so continued to do till it came to the mouth of the sepulchre, where it fell in and I saw it no more." The experience of Christian has been repeated in the lives of tens of thousands of men and women. At the foot of the Cross they have found forgiveness and peace. The greatest novelists have joined with Bunyan in proclaiming this truth.

Nathaniel Hawthorne, in his powerful book, *The Scarlet Letter,* relates a drama that was enacted in a little Massachusetts community years ago. A young and beautiful woman was found guilty of transgressing the marriage law. According to the grim Puritan code she should have been doomed to receive the brand of a red-hot iron upon her forehead. A plea for mercy, however, caused a scarlet letter on her dress to be substituted. If the guilty man had been discovered the penalty, for him, would have been death on the scaffold. But neither the pleas of friends nor the threats of enemies could wring the name of her partner in sin from the lips of the young woman. She chose to bear in her heart the burden of another's agony as well as her own.

All the while, young Dimmesdale, the guilty man, lived in the community loved and honored; but not for a moment, night or day, did he have peace. He was tormented incessantly by a guilty conscience.

Then one day, into the little Puritan town came the hateful husband of the woman. Disguised as a physician he discovers young Dimmesdale's guilty secret and proceeds to stretch him daily upon the rack of mental torture. Relentlessly he pursues the youth until, worn by remorse and grief, his health breaks down. By a last noble resolve he decides upon full confession. On Election Day, with the Governor of the Colony and other notables in the public square, Dimmesdale strode to the pillory and climbing the scaffold declared to the startled multitude that he was the guilty man who should have stood seven years earlier beside the woman who had borne the brand of shame alone.

His enemy and torturer, seeing him about to confess, cried: "Madman, what doest thou? All shall be well. I can yet save thee." But Dimmesdale, triumphant over sin, replies: "Tempter, thou art too late. With God's help I will escape thee." To which his enemy replied: "In all the world there was no place so secret; no high place, nor lowly place where thou couldst have escaped me save this scaffold."

How true to life is Hawthorne's moving story. In confession and repentance alone may deliverance be found. It speaks a message to every man and woman who has experienced the deceptive power of sin; who has been crushed beneath a load of guilt; whose awakened conscience has almost driven him mad. There is no place in the world so secret as to hide him. He may "take the wings of the morning and dwell in the uttermost parts of the sea," but even there he will make his bed in Hell, for remorse will still be his companion. There is but one refuge where he may escape the enemy of his soul, and that is the Cross, the Cross of Calvary where there is healing and forgiveness for all wounded, bleeding, and broken hearts.

Finally, in the Cross of Christ we have a revelation of the Redeeming Love of God.

There was a time when the Atonement was set forth as a sacrificial act upon the part of Christ to appease the wrath of an angry God. Indeed, to a generation of Sunday-school children not so far removed there were given little colored pictures which represented God shooting the arrows of his wrath at a world of sinful men, while Jesus, standing between God and man, caught these arrows into his own heart. That teaching is false and un-Scriptural. It was God who "so loved the world as to give his only begotten Son. . . ." The redemptive purposes of Calvary originated in the heart of God.

There are, of course, those who belittle the conception of a suffering God and who remind us that this teaching is akin to an ancient heresy. They assert that it degrades God to think of his bearing and sharing the penalty that sin inevitably brings upon the sinner. Dr. Fairbairn was nearer the truth, however, when he said: "The theologians never made a greater mistake than when they sought to magnify God by placing him above the battle." If Christianity had possessed no doctrine of the Atonement it would have been compelled to invent one to save the character of

God; for the woman of the street who willingly perishes in the gutter, wrapping her garments about her little child to save its life, would be morally superior to a God who continued to exist in a state of perpetual bliss, unmindful of the tragedies and sufferings which involved his creatures.

Many years ago I read an essay which, I believe, was written by the Reverend S. D. Gordon. He related an incident which gives to us a beautiful representation of the meaning of the Cross. He tells of a minister whose boy Philip had caused him much sorrow. The father pleaded with the lad and warned him but to no avail. Finally, he told the boy that if he continued his wrongdoing he would be severely punished. Before many days had passed the father realized that, once again, his son had disobeyed him. What was he to do? If he remitted the promised penalty the result would have been morally disastrous for the boy; so he said to him, "Every night for a week you must leave your little room and sleep on a cot in the attic. I hope that this will cause you to realize your mistake." That night, after the boy had gone supperless to the attic, the minister sat down at the table for his evening meal, but his appetite had vanished. He went into the study to complete some work which he had begun in the morning, but he was unable to concentrate his thoughts. He picked up the evening paper to read, but tears blinded his vision. He went to bed, but he could not sleep for thinking of his boy. Finally, he said to his wife, "I am going to the attic to spend the night with Philip." He went upstairs and lay down on the little cot beside his boy. He found him wide awake. Philip pressed his tear-stained cheek against his father's face and so they passed the night together. Every night of the punishment the father shared it with his boy. We are not surprised to learn that that son, grown into manhood, went forth as a missionary to interpret the vicarious passion of Christ to the people of China.

The incident, which Dr. Gordon relates, is a parable of Calvary. God was in Christ, bearing and sharing the penalty of sin. He took upon himself the burden that ought to have been borne by sinful man. He made our case his own. In the Cross we see not only the awful nature of sin, but also the suffering heart of God. Vicariousness becomes but another name for love. There is only one response that is adequate—the surrender of ourselves without reserve to him in glad and loving submission.

> See, from His head, His hands, His feet,
>   Sorrow and love flow mingled down!
> Did e'er such love and sorrow meet,
>   Or thorns compose so rich a crown?
>
> Were the whole realm of nature mine,
>   That were an offering far too small;
> Love so amazing, so divine,
>   Demands my soul, my life, my all.

THE SIN OF MORAL COWARDICE

And Levi made him a great feast in his own house: and there was a great company of publicans and of others that sat down with them.

ST. LUKE 5:29

THOMAS CARLYLE never wearies of reminding his readers that "in each of us dwells a coward and a hero." The appeal of religion, he suggests, is directed to the hero in us. The truth of that assertion is borne out in the life of St. Matthew. One cannot read the Gospel that has come from the pen of this Evangelist without realizing that he was a brave and candid man. He tells us plainly that he was seated at the receipt of custom when Jesus called him.

The other Evangelists, when they describe the calling of Matthew, use his less familiar name Levi. It would seem as though they wished to draw the veil of secrecy over the fact that he had been chief among the publicans. It is sometimes a most kindly and Christian act not to reveal everything that we know about other people. No sooner has Matthew told us that he was a publican than we know at once of his shameful past.

"Publican" was the name by which tax collectors

were known in Palestine. It was the practice of the Romans to sell to the highest bidder the right of collecting taxes in some of her subject provinces. You may be sure that the men who paid a high price for this privilege did not mean to lose money in the transaction.

Because publicans were the representatives of a race that had conquered the Jews they were treated with scorn and hatred. By their own people they were regarded as apostate and traitors. The best society in Palestine excluded them and they were not permitted to give evidence in a court of law. They were social outcasts. It took no little courage, therefore, for Matthew to admit that he was a publican.

Of course, when he entered the service of Rome he did not intend that his character should be debased by the work he had taken in hand.

But try as he would he could not escape the degrading influences of his calling. He simply had to grind the faces of the poor; to squeeze out of his victims every drop of blood; quieting his conscience by saying that "business is business." He did not dare to think of the widows and the orphans. The debt was due, indeed it was overdue, and it must be paid, even if women and children had to be put up for auction in the slave market.

He was led to this employment by love of money, and frequently he thought of the time when he would be ready to retire. Oftentimes he made plans about a villa that he hoped to establish on the hillside above the Lake of Galilee. From it he would be able to look down upon the blue waters. He would surround the closing years of his life with comfort and peace. Money would do this for him, he assured himself.

There was one thing, however, that Matthew left out of the reckoning: that life's best gifts cannot be bought by money. Money cannot buy love. It can buy only a counterfeit of love which often reveals itself in separation, disillusionment, and pain. The writer of the proverbs spoke the truth when he said: "Better a dinner of herbs where love is than a stalled ox and hatred therewith." Money cannot buy happiness, though many people think that it can. It can buy something that passes for happiness, but is only a spurious imitation of the reality. Money cannot buy peace of mind and heart. If wealth could purchase these inestimable blessings then rich people would be the happiest and most contented in all the world; but the facts do not agree with this conclusion. Statistics show that the proportion of suicides is considerably higher among the well-to-do than it is among the poor.

But Matthew refused to believe this, and as he watched the steady accumulation of his financial resources he assured himself that, no matter how disagreeable many of his duties were, the future would hold for him contentment and peace.

At this time an eventful hour dawned in the life of the Jewish publican. It came about in some such a way as this: he was seated at his custom booth near Capernaum when his attention was attracted by a large group of people. They were gathered around one arrayed in a long white robe, who was apparently addressing them. "Who is that man yonder?" Matthew asked one of his assistants. "That is the Prophet of Nazareth," he responded. "Look after these books," said the publican, "and be sure that you keep a true account. I am going over to listen to him."

It was not difficult for Matthew to make his way through the crowd, because no sooner had people recognized the well-known publican than they drew away from him, feeling that any personal contact with a despised tax gatherer would leave them ceremonially defiled.

Just as Matthew had succeeded in elbowing his way to the front of the throng he heard one of the men standing near the Prophet say to him: "Master, speak to my brother that he divide the inheritance with me. He is not willing to give me my fair share of the patrimony." With an unmistakable look of pity in his eyes Jesus answered: "Man, who made me a judge or a divider over you?" Then turning to the multitude he said:

"Take heed, and beware of covetousness, for a man's life consisteth not in the abundance of the things which he possesseth. There was a certain Galilean farmer who learned this truth at bitter cost. His land was exceedingly fruitful so that his barns would not hold the crops that he had grown. 'I will pull them down,' he said to himself, 'and build them bigger still, and then I will say to my soul: "Soul, thou hast much goods laid up for many years, take thine ease: eat, drink and be merry." ' "

For a moment the Nazarene paused and looked into the faces of the people hanging upon his every word; then he added: "That very night the hand of death knocked at the door of his chamber, and he heard God's voice sounding in all the corridors of his being: 'Thou fool, this night thy soul shall be required of thee. Then whose shall those things be which thou hast provided?' "

The stillness of death had fallen over the multitude as the Master concluded He turned and looked at the man whose life had been gripped by the lust for gain and said to him: "So is he that layeth up treasure for himself and is not rich toward God."

That was quite enough for Matthew! He would not listen to any more of such talk. Hurriedly he made his way through the crowd back to the receipt of custom; but he could not deny the fact that he was miserable and unhappy. He knew that the Galilean was right. Turning to his books he began to reckon up, once again, his fast-accumulating resources; but this time they brought no happiness to him. Across the page a sentence was written in letters of fire: "So is he that layeth up treasure for himself and is not rich toward God."

For weeks a battle raged in the soul of Matthew the publican. All day long the words of the Galilean rang in his ears and at night they disturbed his sleep. One day as he was seated in his booth counting out gold and silver, and making entries in his ledger, a shadow fell across his books. Glancing up, he found himself looking into the eyes of the Galilean Prophet. "Matthew," said Jesus, "leave all this and follow me." Although the words were spoken in tenderest accents, there was something tremendously compelling about this Man. For one fleeting moment there loomed up again the vision of that villa by the Sea of Galilee, and years of contentment and ease, but it passed. Now he can see only the face of one whom, at last, he is ready to call "Master." Hurriedly he transfers his duties to a subordinate; prepares a complete statement for the Roman authorities, and then, locking up his presses and closing his books, he leaves all and follows Jesus.

Day by day such happiness came to Matthew as he had never dreamed of before he met the Master. He never tired of looking into that dear, dear face or of listening to him who had brought to his life joy and peace.

Matthew, during the period in which he had served as a publican, had accumulated no small store of this world's goods. After his conversion he was busily employed righting the wrongs that he had previously done. Then one day the idea came to him to summon together, at a great banquet, all his former friends and acquaintances, and to invite Jesus as the guest of honor. Matthew had a twofold purpose in planning this feast: first, it would afford him an opportunity to announce to his friends that he had accepted a new allegiance; that he had become a disciple of Jesus. Matthew once again reveals the fact that he was no coward. He was neither afraid nor ashamed to declare his loyalty to the Nazarene. By making that declaration he would strengthen his own convictions.

I recall an interview which I had some time ago at the close of a Sunday-evening service. A young man waited to talk with me. He had served as a combatant throughout the whole of the Great War. On his return to civil life he had become cynical and disillusioned. Something in the sermon had deeply touched him. In the presence of God he confessed to deep-seated wrongs in his life; sins that were destroying his efficiency and marring the happiness of his home. He resolved to make a new beginning. Like Matthew of old he rose up and followed Christ. As he shook hands with me that night he said, "I am going back to the hotel now to tell the boys with whom I have been traveling for years that I am through with the old life."

That young man knew the value of a definite, resolute, and courageous beginning. No one would be in any doubt as to where he stood. Matthew, also, intended that this should be true of him.

There was a second reason why he gave this banquet to his acquaintances. He wanted them to see and to meet his new-found friend.

With a happy heart Matthew told Jesus of his plans and invited him to be the chief guest at the feast. "Whom else have you invited?" Jesus asked. Immediately Matthew's face fell. "I'm sorry, Master," he said. "I did not think of that. You see, the only friends I have had since I've been a tax gatherer have been rather disreputable people. I hadn't any right to invite you to the banquet."

Have you noticed in our text the reserve of Luke? "There was a great company of publicans and of others that sat down with them," he said. "Publicans and of others." Who were the "others"? You have only to read the Gospels to discover that they were the outcasts of society. How often we read of "publicans, harlots and sinners." It was a motley crew drawn from the dregs of society that would meet around Matthew's board. But Jesus, looking kindly at his downcast disciple, said, "It's all right, Matthew. I shall be very glad to be your guest at the supper."

Do you think that it was wise of Jesus to accept that invitation? Immediately, he laid himself open to the criticism of the religious leaders. The Scribes and Pharisees asked, "Why do ye eat and drink with publicans and sinners?" Now, they declared, you know what kind of a man he is. "Birds of a feather flock together."

Why did Jesus accept the invitation in these circumstances? First, because he was the soul of gentlemanly courtesy. He appreciated Matthew's effort to do him honor. Not for worlds would he have hurt the feelings of a disciple. And, in the second place, the Master was happy to have another opportunity of meeting with people who sorely needed his friendship. In justification of his action he answered the Scribes and Pharisees by saying: "They that be whole need not a physician, but they that are sick. I came not to call the righteous, but sinners to repentance."

What interesting reading it would make if we should come upon a report of that night's proceedings—Matthew's tribute to Jesus at the table and the reply which our Lord made. I am sure that there was nothing in the words of Jesus to put a damper on the spirits of the guests at the banquet. The only sermon he preached was the unspoken message of his own radiant personality. Everyone present knew that here was One who possessed the secret of a victorious life, and they felt themselves irresistibly drawn to him.

As we think of the damaged souls that attended Matthew's banquet we cannot help wondering whether or not a certain woman was present who, at a later date, fell down at the feet of Jesus as he sat at dinner in Simon's house and bathed his feet with tears and dried them with the hairs of her head. It is quite possible that she first looked into the face of our Lord as he sat with his disciples in Matthew's home.

Does the incident which we have been studying this morning shed any light upon the perplexing problems of modern life? In a society that cares nothing for Christian ideals, what is a disciple of Christ to do? If, among your acquaintances and mine, there are prevailing practices which we cannot reconcile with Christian conduct, does this mean that we ought to remain aloof from society?

That, exactly, was what some followers of Christ began to do about the fifth century of the Christian era. Monastic life had its commencement then. Christians became ascetics and recluses. They fled away from a world that disowned their Master and his teaching. It was at this time that the famous "Pillar Hermits" appeared. The most noted of these was St. Simeon Stylites. At thirty years of age he built a pillar six feet high, and on top of it he took up his abode. He continued to build pillars higher and higher until, after ten years, he reached a height of sixty feet. For thirty years he lived on the top of this gigantic pillar without ever descending. From many parts of the ancient world people came to see this holy man who had separated himself from the society of his fellows.

No man can justify such an attitude from the teaching of Jesus. His own example in accepting an invitation to Matthew's banquet reveals the fact that he did not run away from life. He taught his disciples that they were to go into human society as redeeming influences. "I pray not," said Jesus, "that thou shouldest take them out of the world, but that thou shouldest keep them from the evil." "Ye are the light of the world," said the Master. "Men do not light a candle and put it under a bushel; but on a candlestick, and it giveth light unto all that are in the house. Let your light so shine before men, that they may see your good works, and glorify your Father which is in heaven." Jesus intended his disciples to be centers of illumination in a dark and sordid world.

Again our Lord said: "Ye are the salt of the earth." The function of salt is to preserve certain things from decay. Jesus tells his disciples, then, that they must go into an evil world and make it wholesome. That was the mission of the Master himself, and he declared it also to be the duty of his disciples.

It is at exactly this point where modern Christians most frequently fail. Christians today do not hesitate to mix with people, but the tragedy is that they are not lights to lighten dark places. They are not like salt, cleansing and wholesome in their influence. They become exactly like those with whom they associate. They accommodate themselves to the standards of those who are about them. They are like the chameleon—a creature that changes its color according to its environment. They are guilty of the sin of moral cowardice.

Those who were at Matthew's banquet could not fail to notice that, during the course of the evening, our Lord did not once modify his conversation or his conduct to the company around him. Jesus at Matthew's table was the same Jesus who knelt at night on the lonely quiet of a Galilean hillside talking with his Heavenly Father. He did not allow the society that surrounded him to pull him down to its level. Rather his influence and example lifted all others up to a higher plane.

God pity the modern Christian who salves his conscience with the vain slogan: "When you are in Rome do as the Romans do." That may be good enough in the case of some trifling convention; but in all vital matters of conduct, whether you are in Rome or New York, do right. We need more convinced, courageous, outspoken Christians today—men and women who are not ashamed to declare their allegiance; who will nail their colors to the masthead; who will go into human society not as vacillating, compromising, apologetic weaklings, but as men and women whose fearless stand for righteousness will bear witness that, like Matthew the publican, they have left all and followed Christ.

A NOBLE KING AND HIS SUCCESSOR

Now the days of David drew nigh that he should die; and he charged Solomon his son, saying, I go the way of all the earth: be thou strong therefore, and shew thyself a man; and keep the charge of the Lord thy God, to walk in his ways . . . that thou mayest prosper in all that thou doest.

I KINGS 2:1-3

WHAT a remarkable Book is the Bible! Upon every segment of human life it sheds a revealing light. As we think today of the sorrow that overshadows not only the British Empire, but the whole English-speaking world, we turn instinctively to the Bible for comfort and guidance.

The words of our text describe the death scene of one of the greatest kings of Israel. True, the record of King David was disfigured by dark passages and ugly blots, but even the moral failures which marred his life served as a foil to set forth in brighter colors his courage, his rare nobility, and his intense spirituality, which were evident whenever he was true to his better self.

He was the first king of Israel to bind the Hebrew people into a great and united nation; and when, at last, death was about to lift from his head the royal crown, he intrusted the throne to his son, Solomon, as his successor, uttering the memorable words of our text: "I go the way of all the earth: be thou strong therefore, and shew thyself a man; and keep the charge of the Lord thy God, to walk in his ways . . . that thou mayest prosper in all that thou doest."

One cannot but feel that, had the opportunity been given to the late King George to offer a charge to his son and successor, Edward, he would have used words very similar to those employed by King David.

Seldom in history has such a wave of deep emotion swept over the British Empire as was evoked a few days ago, when the news was flashed around the world that King George had died. The feeling that stirred in the breast of millions of his subjects was not a perfunctory sorrow for the ruler of an empire, but rather a sense of personal loss, as though a dear friend had gone.

Not always did the character of British kings call forth the admiration and love of their people. There were many occasions on which the death of British monarchs brought to the nation not sorrow, but a feeling of relief and thankfulness.

In the Parchment Room of the British Museum in London, hangs a document yellow and shriveled with age. Little wonder that it is faded, for it is more than seven hundred years old, and is one of the four remaining copies of the original Magna Charta. It is given an honored place in that museum, because it is a symbol of freedom. This is the historic document that was wrested, by the barons of England, from the reluctant hand of King John.

Year after year, he had continued to inflict upon

his subjects one injustice after another. He compelled them to labor at the building of roads, and bridges, and castles, but gave them no recompense for their work or for the materials that were used in construction. In order to enforce his unjust exactions, he used his bodyguard of mercenaries, hired foreign soldiers, to oppress the English people, and he rewarded these hirelings with high offices in the Government.

Scandal after scandal became known regarding his personal life. He was guilty of unpardonable offenses against some of the noblest of his followers. William de Braose he drove into exile, imprisoning and starving his wife and son, because they knew that the King had murdered his own nephew, Arthur. No Englishman, in that day, could be sure of justice or the safety of his person, because of the despotic power of the King.

The smoldering resentment of King John's subjects suddenly burst into flame. On the broad green meadow of Runnymede, he was compelled to pledge to his people that freedom which he had hitherto so resolutely denied.

One of the paragraphs of Magna Charta signed by John provides for the protection of the life, liberty, and property of all free men and guarantees that justice will not be sold, denied, or delayed to any of the King's subjects. The English monarch signed that document and placed the royal seal upon it. There was laid in that hour the cornerstone of an edifice which, through the centuries, has grown into a mighty temple of human freedom.

It was not, however, until the accession of Victoria, in the year 1837, that the English monarchy gathered to itself not merely the devotion and loyalty of its subjects, but their affection and love. Early in the morning of June the twentieth of that year, almost exactly one hundred years ago, Victoria was aroused from her sleep by her attendants, who told her that the Archbishop of Canterbury and the Lord Chamberlain were waiting to speak to her. She received them in evident confusion. They greeted her with the words, "Your Majesty." By that token she knew that she was queen. They informed her that, during the night, William IV had died. When she had recovered from her agitation, Victoria turned to the Archbishop of Canterbury, and said, "I ask your prayers on my behalf." In such a spirit of deep humility, and in dependence on Divine Providence, she commenced her great and glorious reign.

Shortly after this came a day when the windows of St. James' Palace were thrown wide open and Victoria stood there with the members of the royal family and the leaders of State. She was dressed in black. Out in front of the palace, tens of thousands of people were gathered. One of the officials of State stepped forward and proclaimed this girlish person, eighteen years of age, "our only ruler and rightful liege lady, Victoria the First, Queen of Great Britain and Ireland, Defender of the Faith."

The moment that announcement was made, the massed bands struck up the national anthem, the guns in the palace and the Tower thundered a salute, and the cheers of tens of thousands of people rent the air. It was too much for the young Queen; she broke down and buried her face in her mother's bosom.

Mrs. Browning, writing of that incident, says:

> God save thee, weeping Queen!
> Thou shalt be well-beloved.
> The tyrant sceptre cannot move
> As those pure tears have moved.
> The nature in thy eyes we see,
> Which tyrants cannot own,
> The love that guardeth liberties.
> Strange blessing on the nation lies,
> Whose sovereign wept,
> Yea, wept to wear a crown.

The incidents of her reign are too familiar to require recounting here. The words of the historian may well summarize her achievements: "She received a crown that had too often been tarnished by ineptitude and vice. She wore it for sixty-three years, and made of it the symbol of private virtue and of public honor." As Tennyson says:

> Her court was pure; her life serene;
> God gave her peace; her land reposed;
> A thousand claims to reverence closed
> In her as Mother, Wife and Queen.

The noble tradition of monarchy established by Victoria was carried on by her son, Edward VII, and in an even more marked degree by her grandson, the late George V.

Walter Lippmann, addressing the students and faculty of the University of California, said: "We are living today in the midst of one of the revolutionary periods of human history." That is undoubtedly true. Before our eyes empires have been destroyed, and thrones have crumbled. In Europe alone, since the Great War four ruling houses have been overthrown: in Germany, the House of Hohenzollern; in Spain, the Bourbons; in Austria, the Habsburgs; in Russia, the Romanoff Dynasty. In all these countries tourists may wander today through glorious palaces that were once the homes of kings and emperors but are now public museums. There you may see beds in which royalty slept; thrones on which they sat; ballrooms in which they gave their costly receptions; tables, still sparkling with gold and silver plate, at which they celebrated their sumptuous feasts.

Within the last eighteen years, all these dynasties have been swept away; but through the reverberations of the Great War and the unrest of the world-wide economic depression that followed it—two cataclysms that shook the foundations of Western civilization—the throne of Great Britain has remained undisturbed, "broad-based upon a people's will." The credit for this achievement must go, in large measure, to the late King George V.

Few, if any, among the rulers of Britain have understood his people as well as did he. He gained the respect and the affection of all classes. He was one with them in their sorrows and in their joys. Those who are in a position to know tell us that he possessed unusual powers of statesmanship and that, at the Imperial Conference which met in the year 1926, when the representatives of South Africa, of Canada, and of Ireland went to that Conference in a disgruntled frame of mind, it was the tact, diplomacy, and wisdom of King George which happily solved problems that might easily have led to the disruption of the Empire had his attitude been the unreasoning one of a predecessor in the kingly office, George III.

One cannot think, too, of the late King without remembering that religion always exercised a compelling influence upon his life. He attended services of worship with unfailing regularity. We learn, on his own confession, that from his boyhood he made a practice of reading the Bible every day. Only a few years ago he paid this high tribute to the sacred Volume: "The English Bible is the first of our national treasures, and, in its spiritual significance, the most valuable thing that this world affords."

Who can measure the influence, upon the character of the British people, of the sane and wholesome home life of the late King George and Queen Mary? Although he lived in the searching light of high public office, no breath of scandal ever touched his home. All the world honors him today for the qualities that marked his character.

When the King was rapidly sinking, he called for his private secretary, and asked, "How is it with the Empire?" "It is well with the Empire, Sir," the secretary replied. The King smiled and closing his eyes drifted into unconsciousness. A few hours later he died.

What shall we say of his successor, Edward VIII? Will an expectant world witness, in his career, the fulfillment of the charge made by David to his son Solomon: "Be thou strong therefore, and shew thyself a man; and keep the charge of the Lord thy God, to walk in his ways . . . that thou mayest prosper in all that thou doest."

Certainly this, at least, can be said: no British King

ever went to the throne on so high a tide of popular affection as Edward VIII; nor has there ever been a monarch in history more conversant with the aspirations of his people than he. While he was yet Prince of Wales, he visited all parts of the Empire, and won the admiration and love of his subjects. He has been an emissary of good will to other nations, as well.

We recall today, too the reckless abandon with which he risked his life in France to share the lot of the Allied soldiers. On many occasions he was seen trudging along in the battle area, sometimes mud bespattered, as he cheered the soldiers in their monotonous task. Some of the men who went out from these shores, in the American Army, freely to offer their lives in France, will ever remember an occasion when, in the darkness of the night, lighted only by the occasional flare of a star shell, they were stopped by a slim figure dressed in the uniform of a British officer, who said, "Say, chummy, can you give me a light?" Not until hours afterwards did they know that they had been talking with the Prince of Wales.

When Kitchener remonstrated with the Prince about the risk that he was taking in going to France, he replied, "Have I not four brothers?"

While he was in Canada, just prior to his visit to this country, there occurred a simple incident which, nevertheless, revealed the quality of the man. He was inspecting a body of troops near the City Hall in Toronto. His interest was arrested by a group of crippled veterans, with whom he began to talk. While he was conversing with one of these, a sudden gust of wind blew off the man's cap. Like a flash, before anyone had a chance to move, the Prince chased down the long file of men standing at attention, retrieved the veteran's cap, and, in the presence of scores of thousands, placed it again on the man's head.

I am sure that many of you who listen to me this morning will recall the visit of the Prince of Wales to Washington and to New York in the fall of 1919. As he drove through the streets of this city, tens of thousands of people eagerly cheered the youth who, by his modesty and unfailing friendliness, had caught the imagination and won the affection of the people of this great country. Nothing could exceed the warmth of his welcome to New York. On his return to Canada, the Prince of Wales referred to the embarrassment he had felt, because of the honors that had been heaped upon him here. He said, laughingly, "They Princed me so much, that at any moment I expected to bark."

Surely today is a fitting time to recall the tribute that he paid to this nation: "I always feel happy amongst Americans and in American territory," said the present King Edward VIII. "American life appeals to me greatly, and I have many American friends." It is not without significance that this is the man who has now ascended the British throne.

Many people in this country, as well as in Britain, are now hoping and praying that the accession of Edward VIII to the throne of the British Empire will draw together, as never before, the great Anglo-Saxon nations of the world. Surely, there never was a time in history when such unity was needed as it is needed today. In many parts of the world there are rumblings of revolution and rumors of war. One after the other we have seen democracies go down in

Europe, and dictatorships take their place. In nation after nation, not only political, but also religious freedom has been wrested from the grasp of the people. Irresponsible and tyrannical rulers threaten, once again, to involve the world in war. Some there are who tell us that democracy is doomed and that dictatorship, either Communistic or Fascist, will eventually replace it everywhere.

Not for a moment do I believe that prophecy. I would remind you of what one of the greatest political writers of the day has pointed out, that while the democratic saplings have gone down in the storm, the old oaks are still standing. Britain, France, Switzerland, Norway, Sweden, Canada, the United States, and other nations as well, maintain their free institutions. It is significant, too, that world leadership is still in the hands of the democratic peoples of the earth, and please God it shall there remain.

Surely it is an omen that promises well for the future that, in the very hour when Edward VIII ascends the throne of Britain, the last barrier to unity in the naval policies of Britain and the United States has been swept away, and, in the face of a common peril, these two nations are drawing ever closer together. So long as they are in agreement, the world can be saved from irretrievable disaster.

In the midst of a world of unrest and revolutionary ferment, the British throne stands today a mighty bulwark of democracy and freedom.

I refuse to believe that the people of this great Republic or of the British Commonwealth of Nations will ever bow their necks to the yoke of Fascism or Communism, with their denial of liberty, their mass murders, their secret assassinations, and their civil wars. But rather, cherishing a common heritage of freedom, will they labor side by side for the establishment of righteousness and justice among the nations, and of peace and good will to all the children of men.

AVOIDING A BREAKDOWN

Come ye yourselves apart . . . and rest a while.
MARK 6:31

THESE words of Jesus were spoken to his twelve disciples after their return from a preaching mission. They had been in conflict with the forces of evil. They had cast out demons and healed the sick. Everywhere, they preached that men should repent. While they were separated from the Master news reached them that John the Baptist had been brutally done to death by Herod, the King.

When the disciples came back to Jesus they were wearied as a result of an exacting ministry. They were frightened by the news that they had heard about John. It was a band of restless, exhausted, nervous men who stood face to face with him and recounted all that they had taught and done. Looking with understanding eyes at these men, spent and toil-worn, Jesus said: "Come ye yourselves apart . . . and rest a while." "For," St. Mark adds, "there were many coming and going, and they had no leisure so much as to eat."

Jesus' prescription for tired, fretted people is rest and meditation in some quiet place.

If ever there were an age that needed the advice which Jesus gave to his disciples, surely it is ours. Two characteristics of Western civilization are noise and speed. Both of these are destructive of nervous energy and peace of mind. Modern science has immeasurably quickened the pace of human life. Never before were human beings transported from one place to another in so short a space of time. Last year the *Normandie* crossed the Atlantic in less than four and a half days. Sir Malcolm Campbell has driven his motorcar an average speed of three hundred and one miles per hour—five miles a minute. Howard Hughes has made an aeroplane journey across this continent, from the Pacific to the Atlantic, in nine hours and twenty-seven minutes. Within twelve months all these records will have been shattered.

A little more than a week ago I took up a railway time table; on its cover, blazoned in red letters, were these words: "Three hours faster." This time table reminded me of my first visit to New York some years ago. I talked at that time with a director of one of the broadcasting stations here. He mentioned the fact that in this city life is lived at a pace that is probably faster than in any other part of the world. Then he told me this story:

"An official of the Japanese Government visited me in New York to look into the progress that we had made in radio. He wished to travel on the subway, as he had never had that experience; so I took him from a remote part of the city to Times Square. En route we changed from the local to the express. As we were stepping off the train at Times Square, the Japanese visitor asked, 'Why did you change trains?' I said,

'Well, you see, we saved two minutes by that change.' The Japanese looked up quickly, with his inscrutable Oriental expression, and inquired, 'Now what do you propose to do with them?'

"Do you know," said the director to me, "I had never even thought of that."

We imperil our lives today to save two minutes of time, and then we don't know what to do with them. Not only are people subjected to constant strain today by the speed of traffic about them, but life itself in the Western world is organized on an intensively competitive basis. It starts in childhood. Oftentimes, in our educational system, boys and girls are pushed ahead at a rate that little minds and bodies cannot endure. Competition is even more marked in high schools and universities.

I recall a race for first position on the part of two classmates of mine in the final year of Collegiate. On graduation day a delicate, white-faced lad walked forward to receive the gold medal that he had won. His parents were intensely proud of him. His father confided to me, "He has been studying too hard. He has worked many nights until one in the morning." Three months later the boy was dead. The doctor said his death was caused by overstrain of a naturally weak constitution.

How much more is this true of the business world! We hear of "high-pressure salesmanship," "gearing up efficiency," "getting results." W. F. Osborne has said:

> How full our communities are of men who are flinging themselves on life with such preternatural, such demonic

energy, that they are wringing themselves almost habitually dry, so that, in a word, they have nothing but the dregs of their time, energy and temper for their wives and children. Here, surely, is a national and racial menace.

It is little wonder that an element of strain is introduced into the home. Nothing that we may give to our loved ones in the way of material comforts can ever atone for the lack of an atmosphere, in the home, where the heart is mellowed and where love and peace may abide.

I wonder if we are not paying too high a price in health and happiness for financial and material gain? The ancients used a refined method of torture. They bound and shackled a prisoner in a dungeon so that he was held constantly in one position, while a single drop of water fell at intervals upon his unprotected head. Invariably the victim went mad. There is a strain something akin to this in modern life.

Have you ever taken the time to look at the faces of people as they hurry past some pivotal point in this city, such as Fifth Avenue at Forty-second Street? You will see, here and there, some happy faces and some apparently carefree people; but you will see, also, many discouraged faces, and some that have become hard and cynical.

Charles F. Andrews, that devoted servant of Christ in India, tells us that after a long absence in the East he came back to our Western civilization and visited New York. He gave himself especially to the study of people. This is what he found. "There was a strained look on faces where peace ought to have had its throne. The loss of balance in those who had forced the pace to the bitter end was ominously plain. There was also a heart-emptiness where the fever had burnt itself out."

Any medical practitioner will tell you that all around us in this city there is to be found, in the lives of men and women, evidence of marked nervous strain. The symptoms are all too apparent: irritability with people, shortness of temper, morbid timidity and discouragement, habitual cynicism or sadness, minds dominated by the twin enemies of human well-being: worry and fear.

Dr. Alexis Carrel, in his book *Man the Unknown*, points out that mental and nervous troubles have become today an acute problem. While he stresses the part that heredity inevitably plays in these ills, he declares that the disordered lives of modern people are largely responsible for this lamentable condition. He says that one in every twenty-two persons in New York State has spent some time in a mental hospital and that, if the number of admissions continues at the present rate of increase, one million of the children and young men and women who are now in our schools and colleges will ultimately be confined in asylums.

It would seem, therefore, that the clamant need of the hour is for something to come into our lives to give us mental balance, tranquillity of soul, and peace.

It was in a condition of personal disharmony that the disciples returned to Jesus. They were suffering from taut nerves and weary bodies. To them he said:

"Come ye yourselves apart . . . and rest a while." How often the word "apart" occurs in the New Testament: "Jesus departed into a desert place *apart*." "He went up into a mountain *apart*." "Then came the disciples to Jesus *apart*." "And he said unto them: Come ye yourselves *apart* . . . and rest a while." Not only have we here Jesus' advice to people who had been laboring under nervous strain, but we have also revealed the source of the Master's untroubled peace of mind and heart.

Surely if anybody should have broken down under the pressure of life's demands it should have been Jesus. He was moving constantly in the midst of multitudes that crowded out to him from the communities of Galilee and Judea. As he made his way through the crooked streets of Oriental towns, the sick, the blind, the lame, the fever-stricken, the lepers were brought to him. Hour by hour he was in constant touch with loathsome and contagious diseases.

George Adam Smith in his *Life of Henry Drummond* says of that virile Christian: "His sympathy continued to be about him, as it were, the walls of a quiet and healing confessional, into which wounded men and women crept from the world, dared 'To unlock the heart and let it speak'—dared to tell him the worst about themselves."

Once Drummond said to a friend: "Such tales of woe I've heard in Moody's inquiry room that I have felt I must go and change my very clothes after the contact."

But how much more true was this of the Master

to whom men and women came in throngs and, one by one, laid upon his heart the burden of their sins.

No man can render a service that is helpful unless it costs him something. Jesus paid dearly as he ministered to the multitudes. Yet, amid all that accumulation of human wretchedness, surrounded by surging masses of people, sick in body and soul, in the midst of a constant ferment of excitement, Jesus moved always with undisturbed poise, perfectly tranquil and serenely calm. At times he was physically weary to the point of exhaustion. Not for one moment, however, was there any outward indication of this, because inwardly he was always at peace.

"Come ye yourselves apart," said Jesus, "and rest a while." The Master, himself, was constantly drawing upon hidden resources. Every morning, no matter how urgent were the demands upon his time, he would go off to some quiet place to commune with God; and, oftentimes, after the disciples had gone to their rest, he would steal away to the lonely silence of some Galilean hillside. There, with only the stars above him shining brightly in the Syrian sky, he would lift up his face to their light and say "Father," knowing that his voice was heard. There the burden was laid down. There the tides of Almighty God flowed into his soul. There he drew from the Fountainhead of spiritual power such strength as enabled him to go back on the morrow to the multitude and minister again to clamorous human needs.

What a transformation would come over our lives were we to follow our Lord's advice. Then could we remain undisturbed and constant in spirit despite the strain of modern life. We cannot excuse ourselves by saying, "It is impossible for me to get away from the crowded city to the quiet of a mountain side," for Jesus said that we may find God when we have closed the door of our own chamber and looked up, in secret, into his face.

Says George Gissing: "All the great deeds of a spiritual kind have been performed by those who have learned to lead a life of thoughtful silence." There is a definitely therapeutic or healing value in retirement and meditation. From such experiences comes the inspiration for nobler living.

Dr. Jowett never ceased to emphasize this truth. He said: "Get a man who is restfully intimate with the Lord, and you have a man whose force is tremendous." The great preacher's own life was a convincing example of this. In the midst of the pressure of his morning study he turned aside each day for a period of communion with God.

"Be still and know that I am God." "They that wait upon the Lord shall renew their strength." Solitude and silence are essential for all those who would "acquaint themselves with God and be at peace."

Of course, what Jesus recommends calls for time, self-discipline, and patience. We must practice the Presence of God.

An engineer, who worked for some time in far-off Churchill on the Hudson Bay in Northern Canada, related to me an impressive incident. One night, he said, he was listening to his radio. He heard calls from ships at sea; songs, dance music, selections by a symphony orchestra; a few snatches of oratory. As he listened lazily to the programs that crowded the air, suddenly his wandering thoughts were arrested. He was all attention now, listening with great excitement, for he had just heard repeated *his own name*. The announcer at a Winnipeg station was reading an important message to him from a friend.

That is a parable of the beginner at prayer. It is hard to focus your attention. Messages are crowding in: memories of the past; whisperings of the subconscious mind; the clamor of ambition; business anxieties and personal worries. But if you persevere, one day all other sounds will be disregarded for you will hear your own name. God will speak to you. Base your communion upon the Scriptures. Do not feel that you must complete a chapter at each sitting. Read along until you come to a verse that arrests you as God's message to you for that day. Stop right there even though you have read but three verses. Let that living Word of God search your conscience and it will not be long until prayer will begin to rise like a fountain in your heart. When that experience is yours you will rather begin the day without food than omit this period of meditation in the Presence of God. It will bring to you, as it did to Jesus and his disciples, quietness, serenity, power, and peace. You will become a source of strength and inspiration in the midst of a multitude of disoriented lives. "Come ye yourselves apart . . ." says Jesus, "and rest a while."

The message of our text is embodied in the words which are written over the door of the chapel in the central Y.M.C.A. in Tottenham Court Road, London:

Here is a quiet room.
Pause for a little space
And in the deeping gloom
With hands before thy face
Pray for God's grace.

Let no unholy thought
Enter thy musing mind.
Things that the world hath wrought
Unclean, untrue, unkind,
Leave these behind.

Pray for the strength of God;
Strength to obey His plan.
Rise from your knees less clod
Than when your prayer began,
More of a man.

THE VICTORIOUS CHRIST

Thanks be to God, which giveth us the victory through our Lord Jesus Christ.

I CORINTHIANS 15:57

IN THE year 1889 Robert Browning, the British poet, died. An impressive funeral service was held in Westminster Abbey on the last day of that year; but Sir Edward Burne-Jones, who was present on that occasion, declares that it was all too somber. The note of grief and regret was dominant. "I would have given something for a banner or two," says Burne-Jones, "and much more would I have given if a chorister had come out on the triforium and rent the air with a trumpet." Who of us, remembering the unconquerable optimism of Browning, would disagree with the British painter? It was the note of a trumpet—challenging, defiant, triumphant—that Burne-Jones wanted to hear that day.

That is exactly the note that should be sounded at an Easter Morning Service, for we are celebrating a victory. This, too, is the reason why I have selected our text of today. It speaks of conquest. It inspires confidence. It is as though St. Paul had put a trumpet to his lips and sounded a ringing blast: "Thanks be to God, which giveth us the victory through our Lord Jesus Christ."

We are celebrating a victory today because Christ, the Captain of our salvation, triumphed over death and the grave.

It is difficult for us, separated from the disciples by nineteen centuries, to imagine the transformation wrought in them by the news that their Master was alive. Their joy was so much the greater because of the depth of the depression into which they had sunk. They had been overwhelmed with grief and dismay. Added to their sorrow, for the death of their beloved Leader, was the realization that they had failed him in his hour of need. They were crushed by a feeling of humiliation and shame for having forsaken him.

On the night of the betrayal one by one they had pledged themselves to stand by their Master even at the cost of their own lives. Under the shadow of Olivet Peter had said to Jesus: "Though I die with thee, I will not deny thee in any wise." So said they all. Then the terrible blow fell. An armed band came upon them and arrested him. He was tried to the accompaniment of unspeakable indignities. In mockery they crowned him with thorns and spat upon him. Tauntingly they killed him. There was no doubt that he was dead. One of the Romans made sure of that by driving a spear into his side. John, the disciple, standing near the foot of the cross, heard his last terrible cry of anguish. Some friends claimed the body. Tenderly and lovingly they lay it away in a rocky tomb. One by one come the disciples for the holy leave-taking. With compassionate eyes they look at the wounds in his hands and feet. Poor, poor dumb mouths they are which, though voiceless, plead for their pity. Jesus is dead. He is done for. His enemies have murdered him. Having made a sad farewell the disciples leave the tomb—dejected, despairing, hopeless.

How must these men have been startled when on Easter morning Mary Magdalene came rushing in with the first news of the Resurrection! One after the other followed the appearances of Jesus to his disciples. The reality of these is placed beyond the shadow of a doubt by the transformation wrought in the disciples themselves. Despairing men were filled with hope. Saddened faces were transfigured with joy. Cowards were changed into heroes. Broken reeds became pillars of iron.

Had Jesus not triumphed over death and the grave there would not be a Christian Church, a New Testament, or a crusade for the establishment of the Kingdom of God on earth; but one more name would have been added to the roll of martyrs who seem to have died in vain.

John Masefield, the British poet laureate, in his play *The Trial of Jesus*, relates a conversation between Pilate's wife and the centurion who superintended the Crucifixion:

Procula. What do you think the man believed, centurion?

Longinus. He believed that he was God, they say.

Procula. What do you think of that claim?

Longinus. If a man believes anything up to the point of dying on the cross for it, he will find others to believe it. . . .

Procula. Do you think he is dead?

Longinus. No, lady, I don't.

Procula. Then where is he?

Longinus. Let loose in the world, lady, where neither Roman nor Jew can stop his truth.

The centurion was right. They crucified him to silence him; to kill his influence; to seal, forever, his lips. But death was powerless to stop him. It simply let him loose in the world where for nineteen centuries he has been challenging and molding the lives of men. "Thanks be to God, which giveth us the victory through our Lord Jesus Christ."

The most remarkable fact about the transformation wrought upon the disciples of Jesus is that none of the circumstances around them was changed. There was no apparent reason why they should have had a sudden accession of courage. The religious authorities were as hostile as ever to the teaching of the Master. They were as ready as ever to send to death any man who professed to be his follower. The power of Caiaphas, the High Priest, was undiminished. The thirst of the mob for blood was still unappeased. It was perilous for these disciples to admit that they had known the Galilean, let alone to proclaim to the world that they were his friends.

How strange, then, is the attitude of Simon Peter when he stands a prisoner before the Sanhedrin which condemned Jesus to death. A notable healing has been wrought. Caiaphas suspects that in some way the disciples of Jesus are responsible. He rises in his place in the Sanhedrin and, turning to the fisherman-disciple, he asks: "By what power or by what name have ye done this?" Then comes, from the lips of the man once so terror stricken as to have denied his

Lord with oaths and curses, the amazing reply: "Be it known unto you, Caiaphas, and to all the people of Israel, that by the name of Jesus Christ of Nazareth, whom ye crucified, whom God hath raised from the dead, even by him doth this man stand here before you whole."

What is the explanation of these remarkable happenings? Just this: the change was not in the circumstances but in the disciples themselves. Inspired by the risen Christ, timid, vacillating, doubting, denying, recreant men had become as bold as lions at bay. Defeated personalities had become victorious. They could say with St. Paul: "Thanks be to God, which giveth us the victory through our Lord Jesus Christ."

Our text touches upon an urgent need in our own day—the need of victory. There are few victorious personalities about us. One of the tragedies of our time is that multitudes of people who have been chasing the mirage of self-satisfaction, self-indulgence, and self-deliverance have gained for themselves not freedom, but debasing servitude; not victory, but humiliating defeat.

Some of you will recall how the news was blazoned out in New York papers in the summer of 1931 that Ralph Barton, one of the most gifted caricaturists of this nation, had taken his own life. I shall give you the story of this tragedy as it is recorded in a religious periodical. Barton's undoubted talents commanded for him international attention and acclaim. Before he died this brilliant man wrote a letter. It is a momentous document because it reveals the emptiness and folly of modern sophistication. We need have no reluctance in examining this document, because the late Mr. Barton wrote it for the public. He records the story of his successes; of the exceptionally glamorous life that he lived; of the honors and affections that were lavished upon him; of the way in which he drained to its dregs the cup of pleasure, oftentimes caring little for the consequences to other lives. Then comes this paragraph, worthy of a place in Dante's *Purgatorio*:

> I have run from wife to wife, from house to house, and from country to country, in a ridiculous effort to escape from myself. In so doing I am very much afraid that I have brought a great deal of unhappiness to those who have loved me. . . . No one thing is responsible for this [suicide] and no one person except myself. . . . I did it because I am fed up with inventing devices for getting through twenty-four hours a day.

Ralph Barton drew many a caricature with his pencil, but the most remarkable portrait that he ever drew was his own, which he put into the last words he ever wrote. Every sentence in the letter was wrung from the soul of one who has come to the end of his inner resources—a defeated, despairing personality. It is the death cry of sophistication.

The clinics of psychiatrists are filled today with men and women who are frantically trying to find physical and mental well-being and peace of mind. Professor J. A. Hadfield of the University of London, England, in his book *Psychology and Morals*, points out the importance of a properly integrated personality. He reminds us that, if a visit were made to a shell-shock hospital, one would see men paralyzed, blind, deaf, dumb, suffering headaches and other severe pains. These physical symptoms do not originate in the body at all but in the mind. He goes on to say that many modern ailments such as neurasthenia, hysteria, anxiety neuroses, phobias, and sex obsessions are all the result of disturbances of the emotional life.

I quote his exact words: "These physical and mental symptoms are due to defects of character. In dealing with the psycho-neuroses the physician is thus compelled to face the moral problems which lie at the root of these disorders."

Everything that the British psychologist has said is seconded in the works of Professor C. J. Jung. Patients from all parts of the civilized world go to Switzerland to see this specialist and to receive treatment for nervous and mental disorders. In his book *Modern Man in Search of a Soul* he declares: "About a third of my cases are suffering from no clinically defined neurosis but from the senselessness and emptiness of their lives. It seems to me, however, that this can be described as the general neurosis of our time."

Some observers may be deluded into the belief that, for the majority of people, life holds a large measure of happiness; but that is not true, and the fault is not with life but with the people. It is the few and not the many who possess inner resources of quietness, serenity, and peace. The life history of many people is a record of conflict, dissension, and turmoil. They can say with Faust: "Two souls, alas, dwell in my breast apart." They are like the one of whom H. G. Wells says: "He was not so much a personality as a civil war."

Take, for instance, the problem of social drinking

to excess and the use of drugs. Why have these habits spread with such rapidity even among intelligent and educated people? It is simply an attempt on their part to escape from life. They have experienced its insipidity and senselessness, and they seek a temporary oblivion in the use of liquor or drugs. It is a make-believe gaiety that they enjoy. They are running away from life. This is a species of moral cowardice that oftentimes has its climax in suicide.

The greatest need of our time is for something to come into the lives of men and women and give to them the victory. People excuse themselves by saying life is so hard or so empty or so tragic that one cannot be blamed for becoming weary of it. So we have a generation of neurotics, with broken homes and shattered lives.

Well, what can we do about it? Is there any remedy? The key to the solution of this baffling problem is found in the words of the text which I bring to you on Easter Sunday morning: "Thanks be to God, which giveth us the victory through our Lord Jesus Christ." What the living Christ did for Simon Peter, Saul of Tarsus, and the whole band of the disciples, he can do for you today. He can give to you victory at the identical place where formerly you have met only defeat.

To me the most convincing evidence of the Resurrection of Jesus is not that which is usually stressed at Easter time. It is not the empty tomb, though that is significant. It is not the appearances to the disciples, important as these are. It is not even the fact that something undoubtedly happened which changed these men from pygmies into spiritual giants. To me the most convincing evidence that the Cross of Calvary did not stop Jesus but merely released him in the world is the transformation which I see being wrought in the lives of men and women, young and old, in New York City today. What I see Christ doing here in this church, as I meet scores of men and women in personal interviews, is of even greater significance to me than what he did in Galilee nineteen hundred years ago.

In the closing moments of this sermon may I give to you the story of one individual whose life illustrates exactly what I have been talking about today? This case is unusual in that I have never met personally the one of whom I speak. I hold in my hand a series of letters written by a young woman twenty-one years of age. Her identity must remain concealed. Every sentence in this correspondence reveals an unusually alert mind. She is a college graduate and holds a teaching position Here is a modern *Pilgrim's Progress*.

The first letter is dated January 20, a year or two ago. It reeks of pessimism and agnosticism. She has lost her religious faith. Discontented and unhappy, she has plunged into dissipation. Like many another she has discovered that the fruit of sinful pleasures is like the apples of Sodom—attractive to behold but filled with ashes. "Your religious beliefs are very abstract," she writes, "but some of the relations that I have are quite concrete." Yet happiness had taken wings. "I have tried everything," she confesses, "and have come to the conclusion that the only way to peace is by the closing of the waters of the river over my head." That, from a girl of twenty-one!

In answer to my reply came a second letter dated February 26. "I am sorry," she writes, "that I cannot tell you that my difficulties are solved." She goes on to say, however, that she is faithfully following the way of prayer that I had suggested, and continuing to seek a new faith and a new way of life.

The third letter is dated April 16. The light at last has dawned. I quote:

> This has been the most joyous Easter of my life. In fact, it has been my first Easter in one sense—the first one of realization. I have found what I sought: the shadow of a great Rock in a weary land. Of course, I realize that the race has yet to be run, but I am sure that I have the strength to carry on without fear wherever life shall lead. And as for happiness, I understand why Christ spoke of "living waters." Every part of life is taking on new life for me and surging up with joy.

The fourth letter, marking the climax of this experience, was written on June 20.

> It would be impossible for me to begin to tell you of the ever-deepening sense of peace and assurance which I have experienced in the past few months. Every smallest thing has taken on new meaning. Life is full to the very brim of joy and gladness. So many things which seemed of tremendous and terrifying importance have dwindled to mere empty nothings. Fear and loneliness, my twin enemies, are gone. When they attack I just come here to my window seat and read Paul's Epistle to the Romans, and at once they are defeated.

Thanks be to God, who giveth us the victory!

Now, look back at the first letter and contrast it

with the last. In one you see a young woman at the end of her inner resources—discouraged, cynical, despairing. Life is not worth living. The last letter reveals a radiant individual triumphing over depression, fear, loneliness, temptation. Like the disciples after the Resurrection she has been transformed by the Spirit of Christ.

Let each of us, on this Easter morning, bow in lowly surrender to that victorious Personality who alone can give to life its supreme meaning, and then we, too, shall be able to cry exultingly with the Apostle Paul: "Thanks be to God, which giveth us the victory through our Lord Jesus Christ."

WHAT IS GOD LIKE?

So God created man in his own image, in the image of God created he him.

GENESIS 1:27

. . . Who being the brightness of his glory, and the express image of his person.

HEBREWS 1:3

THE Reverend Studdert Kennedy, a beloved chaplain in the Great War, tells us that one day he visited a badly wounded soldier in a hospital in France. The man had been terribly mutilated by shell splinters. After they had conversed for a little while, the soldier looked up into Kennedy's face, and said, "Padre, I wish you would tell me what God is like."

I am sure that this desire, even though not audibly expressed, will be found in the hearts of many people. Like Philip on the night of the betrayal we, too, would say: "Lord, show us the Father, and it sufficeth us."

One has only to listen to a group of people discussing this subject to see how varied are their ideas. About a dozen young men belonging to a religious club, in Winnipeg, took this topic for discussion one night. One young man said, "When I try to picture

God I see his face as it is painted by Michelangelo on the ceiling of the Sistine Chapel in Rome, especially in the panel that portrays the creation of man. The face of God is majestic, serene, powerful, and yet full of kindliness and sympathy."

Another said, "I think of God as he is pictured in the sixth book of Milton's *Paradise Lost*. He is seated on a throne, surrounded by legions of angels, and his out-flashing glory fills the whole of Heaven."

Still another said, "I think of God as the sun, so luminous in glory that no eye can behold his face."

But these pictures tell us very little about the nature of God. Let us turn now to our texts to see what light the Bible will throw upon our problem.

In the first text it is recorded that God created man in his own image What are we to understand from these words? Well, some of us can vividly recall the impressions of our childhood. We thought that God gathered together a quantity of dust, or clay, and gradually kneaded or molded it into the shape of a human body, much in the same way that wax modelers, in our own time, knead plastic substances into the likeness of famous men, so that they bear a startling resemblance to the original. Instances of this may be seen in Madame Tussaud's wax works in London.

In other words, we understood this text to mean that man's physical features resemble the God who created him. Indeed, the Bible would seem to support this idea, for does it not speak of the hands of God, the ears of God, the eyes of God, the arms of God, the fingers of God, and the feet of God?

What are we to understand by these Scriptural

references to the features and organs of God? If God possesses all these members, does it not mean that he created man physically after his own likeness? The answer, I think, is perfectly obvious. The Bible speaks of the hands, the face, and feet of God, because the only way that we human beings can think of God at all is in physical terms with which we are familiar.

Let me offer an analogy. Suppose some member of this congregation were to find himself in the heart of Africa, conversing with an ignorant and uncivilized pygmy. Let us suppose that he wanted to describe to this savage what a modern city looks like: to picture such familiar objects as skyscrapers, telephones, radios, automobiles, and aeroplanes. What terms would he use? What could he use, save only those terms with which the pygmy is familiar? He would find himself drawing comparisons from mud huts, jungle birds, bamboo poles, and other such objects as the pygmy could understand. The Bible is constantly doing this for us. It is full of material symbols which represent spiritual reality. Heaven, for instance, is pictured with streets of gold and gates of pearl.

So, too, we fall back upon symbolism when we talk about abstract truth. Dr. Talmage, in one of his sermons, used this sentence: "No sooner have you built your monuments, than time, with mossy fingers, begins to tear them down." Time is here conceived, not as an abstract reality, but as a physical being who, with his fingers, tears down the works of man. Such vivid imagery arrests and impresses us.

When we think about God we are compelled, in a measure at least, to think about him in terms of physical symbols. Are we to believe, then, that man's face, and hands, and eyes, and feet were modeled by the Creator in his own likeness? The late Alexander Whyte, D.D., minister of Free St. George's, Edinburgh, has answered our question:

> In searching in man for the Divine image, we must pass beyond all in him that was made of the dust of the ground, for no formation of dust, not even when it is refined and elaborated into flesh and blood . . . can carry an impression of the image of God. It is not in man's body that the Divine image stands, but in his soul, in his mind, in his conscience, and in his heart.

We have heard, recently, a great deal in our high schools and universities about man's relationship to the animals. It is claimed that you can find bone for bone, muscle for muscle, nerve for nerve, blood vessel for blood vessel in the body of man, identical with those in the higher animals. Undoubtedly there are impressive similarities to be found in such a comparison. The emphasis of recent years, therefore, has been: "Behold, how like an animal man is."

My purpose is quite different from that this morning. I ask you to think, not how like an animal man is, but how like God he is. I would direct your thought to those powers in man which lift him above all created things, and mark him out as a creature apart in the universe.

Says our text: "So God created man in his own image." Does not that suggest an answer to the question which we have set for ourselves this morning? If the soul of man has come from God, and has been made in his image and likeness, then to know man is, in a measure, to know God. The spiritual qualities by which man transcends all other life on earth are the qualities which, to a degree at least, he shares with his Creator. God is a Spirit, and man, essentially, is a spirit, even though God, in his greatness, outshines man as the noonday sun outshines a flickering candle. Yet, according to the Bible, the spirit of man is akin to the Spirit of God and bears the Divine likeness.

God and man, after all, must be essentially alike in both mental and moral qualities, or else there could be neither scientific progress nor spiritual revelation. Let us look at the matter of human progress first. How many of the advances that science has made in the last fifty years would have been possible if the Intelligence that created the universe were inherently different from our own? In that eventuality, man would have been faced with impassable barriers and inscrutable problems. But, instead of this, wherever he has investigated the universe he has found light breaking in upon him. He has been able to plot its laws and to reduce them to intelligible formulas. He has then passed on his limited achievements to those who followed him, and they carried them forward to final success.

What a thrill must have come to that group of scientists who experimented with the spectroscope and witnessed its triumph. They caused the light coming from a star hundreds of millions of miles away to pass through this remarkable appliance and then to be thrown on a screen hanging on the wall. There it was broken up into its constituent colors. The scientists who were watching the experiment saw, with joy, the proof that in those distant heavenly bodies there were lead, copper, iron, and many other minerals that are to be found in our earth.

Wherever man has explored the universe, whether it be the infinite expanse of the heavens observed through the telescope, or the infinitesimal cosmos that the microscope reveals, everywhere he sees unvarying laws operating according to an intelligent plan.

How much more truly can the modern astronomer utter the words that were spoken by Kepler long ago, when he stood on the platform of his observatory at Prague and, sweeping the heavens with his telescope, cried: "O God, I think thy thoughts after thee."

Whatever be the nature of the Power behind the universe that we call God, we know that an infinite Intelligence is there, of which the mind of man is a small model.

There comes to my mind, this morning, the memory of a glorious walk through Glen Sligichan in the Isle of Skye. Beside me was a young Highlander. We journeyed on foot for sixteen miles. After we had traveled half the distance through the Glen, the Coolin Mountains towered, on each side, more than three thousand feet sheer above us. The Glen was deep, dark, and lonely. Far above, we could see the mountain peaks gilded with sunshine, but not a shaft struck into the depth of the valley.

In that hour I experienced the emotions that sweep over a Highlander in his native haunts. The silence of that weird place was broken only by the murmur of a distant stream which, clear as crystal, flowed down the mountain side. There came to my mind the words of Coleridge:

> So lonely 'twas, that God himself
> Scarce seemèd there to be.

I found myself wondering whether anybody else had ever penetrated into that mysterious Glen, when suddenly I caught sight of a boulder, one side of which was worn smooth by the wind and rain. On that surface, a geometrical figure had been drawn. Someone had amused himself by working out a problem in Euclid. The moment I spied that, I recognized the work of mind and knew that somebody had been there before us.

So has it been in the history of scientific progress. Wherever man has turned his telescope upon the starry heavens, no matter how deep he has penetrated into the vast solitudes, everywhere he sees the work of Mind, and he knows that Somebody has been there before him.

With our limited human intelligence, we have but touched the fringe of the mighty wonders with which the Creator has stored his universe. In the years that lie ahead, marvels as yet undreamed of will be revealed to the exploring mind of man.

We can, therefore, say with conviction that, whatever else we know about God, we are certain that he is Infinite Intelligence. The loftiest intellect that the world has ever seen, is but a dim reflection of the Mind of God.

Again, as we have already noted, if there were not a spiritual affinity between God and man, there could be no revelation, inspiration, or communion with God.

Man has been made a moral and spiritual personality in the image of His Creator. This is the message of Tennyson when he sings:

> Speak to Him, thou, for He hears, and
> Spirit with Spirit can meet—

There lies the explanation of prayer. It is the finite spirit of man in communion with the infinite Spirit of God.

This is the source, too, of those majestic precepts that were thundered forth by the prophets of Israel. Their spirits were attuned to the voice of God and, having listened to him, they declared his will for men.

If there had been no kinship between the human and the Divine there could have been no Incarnation. Jesus was the "absolute immanence" of God whose image all men bear.

In the second place, then, we are able to make another positive affirmation about the unseen Creator. We can point to the noblest life in history, apart from Jesus, and say, "That is but a broken light of God."

By observing man we have learned two truths about God. First, God is supreme, unlimited, infinite Intelligence. Secondly, he is the embodiment of moral and spiritual perfection as it is revealed in holiness and love.

But if man were the only source of our knowledge of God we should know very little about him. In man, the image of God has been marred and defaced by sin. It is but a blurred and imperfect likeness that we see. That is the reason why we have selected a second text to supplement the first.

Our first text asserts that God made man in his own image. The second text declares that, in Jesus, may be seen the express image, or perfect likeness of God. Dr. Moffatt makes this especially clear when he translates Hebrews 1:3 as follows: "Reflecting God's bright glory, and stamped with God's own character."

So from man we turn to the Son of Man to learn what God is like. Jesus was fully aware that in his own life and character God was perfectly revealed.

On the night of the betrayal when Philip said to the Master: "Show us the Father and it sufficeth us," did not our Lord answer: "Have I been so long time with you, and yet hast thou not known me, Philip? He that hath seen me hath seen the Father."

In Jesus, we have a revelation of God than which, in human form, none more perfect can be conceived. The late Professor H. R. Mackintosh, of Edinburgh, emphasizes this fact when he says: "The words of Jesus are the voice of God. The tears of Jesus are the pity of God. The wrath of Jesus is the judgment of God. . . . When in secret we look into God's face, still it is the face of Jesus that rises up before us."

We have reached the goal of our quest, to know what God is like, when we come face to face with Jesus, who is "the brightness of his glory and the express image of his person." The image of God, which in man is sullied and defiled, in Jesus is seen in all its pristine splendor.

It will avail us little, however, to know what God

is like if we do not know him in his power and his love. We noted a moment ago that the moral and spiritual endowments of man are the qualities that lift him above all created things. Those endowments are exercised in the fullest measure, only through communion with God. In prayer we are utilizing God's greatest gift to man.

What a tragedy that men and women, made in the image of their Creator, should fail to use those powers that chiefly distinguish them from the animal creation.

> For what are men better than sheep or goats
> That nourish a blind life within the brain,
> If, knowing God, they lift not hands of prayer
> Both for themselves and those who call them friend?

May we resolve this morning to lift up hands of prayer to the God who has created us until, day by day, we shall continue to grow into his image and likeness; and thus enter into a fellowship with him, which not all the ills of life, nor even death itself, can sever.

A DOOR NO MAN CAN SHUT

Behold, I have set before thee an open door, and no man can shut it.

REVELATION 3:8

LAST Sunday morning we centered our minds upon the impressive thought that the old year had almost run out. We looked back along the road by which we had come and heard this message from the Word of God: "Ye shall henceforth return no more that way." We were oppressed with thoughts of opportunities gone beyond recall, of resolutions broken, of kindly deeds unperformed, of aspirations unrealized, of healing words unspoken.

> Of all sad words of tongue or pen,
> The saddest are these: "It might have been."

With the passing of the old year into eternity, it seemed as though we had heard the closing of a door —a door which, by inexorable decree, can never be opened again.

Now, on the first Sunday morning of the New Year, I bring to you quite a different message. Originally, the words of our text did not refer to a point of time; and yet they have special significance for us as we stand today on the threshold of another year. "Behold, I have set before thee an open door, and no man can shut it." That message is replete with boundless hope. No sooner has one door closed than another opens. The past has gone forever, but the future, full of promise, stretches out before us.

This message of God was spoken, first of all, to the church at Philadelphia in Asia Minor. The open door, doubtless, refers to the strategic position of this Christian Church. Philadelphia was located in the Province of Lydia and was situated almost in the center of Asia. Important highways passed through the city, carrying traffic to the Aegean Sea. The meetings of the Council of the Roman Province of Asia were held here. It was the gateway to the whole Eastern country. Archaeologists, who have been digging in the foundations of this ancient city, have unearthed a strongly built citadel, a theater, luxurious baths, and the ruins of a magnificent temple.

Into that city, with its highly advanced pagan civilization, came, one day in the first century of the Christian era, a few followers of Jesus Christ. They established a Church. It was pitifully small in comparison with the splendor of the heathen temple. But God's message to this Church highly commended it: "Thou hast kept my word, and hast not denied my name." To this body of Christian people, conscious of their insufficiency, came an inspiring challenge: "Behold, I have set before thee an open door, and no man can shut it."

For us, also, this message has special significance as we face the New Year. God has flung wide open to us the door of opportunity. He has placed us in this city, at the crossroads of the world. All the problems of mankind are represented in the multitude which, like a mighty river, rolls unceasingly through the streets of this metropolis.

Situated in the center of all this teeming life, we hear God's commission to us: "Behold, I have set before thee an open door, and no man can shut it." Have we faith, vision, and courage sufficient to respond to this challenge? The task is not an easy one, and there are many adversaries. The most formidable of these is the spirit of secularism. Already, in many parts of this nation, it has robbed the Sabbath Day of its sanctity. No longer is it regarded as a day apart: a day on which the spiritual side of man is given an opportunity for growth and development. It has crept into the Christian Church, so that, in some cases, the pulpit has become a forum for the discussion of contentious political and economic issues. Six days of the week these topics clamor for a hearing and our people have a right to expect a brief respite from them when they assemble to worship God.

The spirit of secularism has made its influence felt, too, in the lives of Church members and officials. Jesus said: "Seek ye first the Kingdom of God and his righteousness; and all these things shall be added unto you." But many, even among his followers, have reversed that teaching. The things are given the first place, and the Kingdom of God and his righteousness are relegated to a secondary position. Temporal plans and individual convenience are given priority, while God, his House, and his Kingdom are allowed whatever happens to remain of the dregs of our time and our interest.

What is it that determines a Christian's presence in the House of God? Is it a sense of loyalty to Christ, so deep and so real that only illness will prevent that attendance? Is it a realization that a scornful world is watching the Church and rejoices at every indication of indifference on the part of those who have espoused its cause? Or is it a matter of personal convenience, a secular counterattraction, a friendly party, or a vagrant cloud with a few drops of rain that determines the matter? If these latter be the deciding influences for fathers and mothers, need we look very far to find the explanation of the indifference of our children? And, in God's name, I ask you what is going to happen to the Church of the next generation?

Many are asking today why the Church oftentimes stands halted, defeated, impotent. May I suggest that the truest explanation will be found if many of us who have named the name of Christ will but look deeply into our own hearts and lives, and probe there the measure of our loyalty to Christ and his Kingdom.

We do well to ponder this morning the Word of God addressed to the Church at Laodicea: "Because thou sayest, I am rich, and increased with goods, and have need of nothing; and knowest not that thou art wretched, and miserable, and poor, and blind, and naked: I counsel thee to buy of me gold tried in the fire, that thou mayest be rich; and white raiment, that thou mayest be clothed, and that the shame of thy nakedness do not appear; and anoint thine eyes with eye-salve, that thou mayest see. As many as I love, I rebuke and chasten: be zealous therefore, and repent."

Give me, in this church, one hundred members who put the Kingdom of God first in everything, and I promise you that from it there will go forth a spiritual power that will shake the city of New York. This is the challenge that God is bringing to us today: "Behold, I have set before thee an open door, and no man can shut it."

The hand of God has set before us today an open door to a new beginning as individuals. New Year has ever been a time of fresh resolve and of renewed consecration. Many people draw up resolutions which they keep before them throughout the New Year, as a constant reminder of a vision of nobler living. To others the thought of New Year's resolutions is a subject only for jest. When should we feel impelled to make a fresh start in life if not in the hour when there is borne in upon us the crushing realization of all our mistakes and failures in the past?

Phillips Brooks strikes a true note when he says: "Sad will be the day for any man when he becomes contented with the thoughts he is thinking and the deeds he is doing; when there is not beating at the doors of his soul some great desire to do something larger which he knows he was meant and made to do!" That will always involve new resolutions. Do you think that it will make no difference to your character if you go on into the New Year satisfied with the meager achievements of the old? Is it a matter of little concern whether or not you pitch your ideals higher than your past achievements have been?

Professor Hocking of Harvard has said: "There is a deep tendency in human nature to become like that which we imagine ourselves to be." Life's experience proves the truth of this assertion. Enter the year telling yourself that you are a slave—manacled and shackled by habits whose grip on your life cannot be broken—and a slave you will remain. Convince yourself that it is quite impossible for you to rise above the low moral and spiritual level of the past, and on that depressed plane you will abide.

Drag with you into the New Year the remembrance of your former follies, blunders, and mistakes, like a convict dragging the ball and chain on his foot, assuring yourself that another year of bitterness and disillusionment will be yours, and it will verily come to pass.

But if, on the other hand, you begin the New Year with resolve that, God helping you, the "low-vaulted past" will be left far behind and a new era of spiritual achievement will open before you, then, by his grace, you will witness the glad consummation of your hopes. That is the glory of the Gospel of Christ. That is the constantly reiterated message of the Scriptures. "The Bible is the most bracing, cheering, and optimistic book in all the world." It brings not a message of barred gates and bolted doors, but of an open door that no man can shut. It speaks of recovery, restoration, redemption, salvation.

When Jesus met with men and women who had been defeated in the past, he did not keep reminding them of their failures. He showed them what, by the grace of God, they might yet become. In effect he said to them: "Behold, I set before thee an open door and no man can shut it." Then, one by one, they entered through that door into the joy and peace of a life that is life indeed.

> I held it truth, with him who sings
> To one clear harp in divers tones,
> That men may rise on stepping stones
> Of their dead selves to higher things.

Finally, before us today stands the open door to a life of fellowship with Christ, so intimate and real that death is powerless to end it.

This Sacrament is the perpetual pledge to us of an unbroken and unbreakable communion with our risen Lord. On the night of his betrayal, when he instituted the Supper, Jesus said to his disciples: "I will not drink henceforth of this fruit of the vine until that day when I drink it new with you in my Father's Kingdom." These words of our Lord assure us that there will yet come a day when the long struggle for righteousness will be crowned with triumph, and life's broken ties will be united again: "When God shall wipe away all tears from our eyes; and there shall be no more death, neither sorrow, nor crying, neither shall there be any more pain: for the former things are passed away."

What a comfort these promises bring to us when we recall the fact that twenty-two members of this church have passed into the Unseen since last we met for a New Year Communion service. They have joined the larger company of the members of the Fifth Avenue Presbyterian Church, ministers and people, who now sit around the Bridal Supper of the Lamb.

I am thinking this morning of a Communion service that was celebrated in Wellington Church, Glasgow, Scotland. This service is recorded in Dr. Morrison's biography. The beloved minister of Wellington Church had been ill for some time. At the Friday night Preparatory service the Reverend J. Stuart Holden of London, well known in our congregation here, declared that the minister was improving. Early Sunday morning, however, there was a relapse. He crossed the river of Death, and "all the trumpets sounded for him on the other side."

As it neared eleven o'clock on Sunday morning, the congregation came streaming up through the pillars at the front of Wellington Church, assembling for a Communion service. The elders met them at the door, and informed the grief-stricken people of the translation of their beloved leader. It was a service never to be forgotten. All eyes were turned toward the vacant chair, in which the congregation had been accustomed to see him who, for twenty-five years, had been their leader in the things of Christ. The Communion hymn was that fine old paraphrase: "Let not your hearts with anxious thoughts be troubled or dismayed." The silence that followed it was broken, here and there, by a half-stifled sob as the elements were distributed. One who was present says: "The glory which streamed through the open door, by which Morrison had gone, lighted up the faces of his people, as they sat around the Table of the Lord." May we, like Morrison's congregation, be conscious of the presence of those who, having passed within the veil, are yet one with us in an unbreakable Communion.

"Behold, I have set before thee an open door, and

no man can shut it"—a door into a life of fellowship with Christ and his people, so intimate and real that death is powerless to end it.

> O Saviour Christ, I pray Thou wilt be near
> To consecrate the newly opening year.
> O, may Thy love omnipotent and free
> Bind every fibre of my heart to Thee.
> And every power and every wish complete
> Be laid in full surrender at Thy feet.

WHAT PREACHING HAS DONE FOR THE WORLD

For though I preach the gospel, I have nothing to glory of: for necessity is laid upon me; yea, woe is unto me, if I preach not the gospel!

I CORINTHIANS 9:16

IN CANADA last year about ten ministers of various denominations ran as candidates in the Federal election. They divided their allegiance among three political parties. Each one believed that the victory of his party would be a contribution to the advancement of God's Kingdom on earth. Apparently, however, they were a long way from a common agreement, for at least two of these parties advocated diametrically opposed social programs.

In most cases these clergymen did not resign from the ministry or from their own local church. They frankly recognized the uncertainty of politics and when they were defeated, as most of them were, they went back to their pulpits again.

Not for a moment would we impugn the motives of these men. They honestly believed that they could make a greater contribution to national righteousness by going into politics than by remaining in the pulpit.

The sincerity of their conviction in this matter, however, could have been demonstrated to better advantage if they had been willing to risk all on their decision. As it is, we are left with the uneasy feeling that the ministry has been relegated to a secondary place.

I mention these facts only because they reveal a conception of the Christian ministry which is separated, from the viewpoint of St. Paul, as far as the east is from the west. He says: "For though I preach the gospel, I have nothing to glory of: for necessity is laid upon me; yea, woe is unto me, if I preach not the gospel!"

Paul believed that God had selected him for this high calling and that he who had chosen him would equip and empower him for the task. This was the belief, too, of all the apostles. It was shared also by the prophets of Israel. One cannot read the life story of these seers and saints without realizing that there was laid upon them a Divine compulsion. They had received an imperious summons from Jehovah, their God. Many of them hesitated and shrank back from the tremendous responsibility placed upon them.

It was so with Moses when he was called upon to become the deliverer of the enslaved Israelites. He replied: "Who am I that I should go unto Pharaoh and that I should bring forth the children of Israel out of Egypt." He pleaded lack of equipment for the task. But under the compelling urge of the Divine Will he accepted his commission.

Then there was Elijah, a man timid by nature, somewhat easily overawed, a simple son of the desert who would have much preferred the solitude of the wilderness to responsible missions in the capital city of Israel. But yet, under the constraint of Jehovah, his God, he goes forth, brave as a lion at bay, to face Ahab and to pronounce the judgments of God upon that apostate monarch.

Again, we see Jeremiah timidly shrinking back from the challenge of God. "O Lord God," he answers, "behold, I cannot speak for I am a child." But the Lord answers him: "Say not, I am a child, for thou shalt go to all that I shall send thee and whatsoever I command thee thou shalt speak. Be not afraid of their faces for I am with thee to deliver thee, saith the Lord."

So was it with all the prophets of Israel, whether it be Isaiah kneeling in reverent awe in the temple; or Amos tending his flocks and herds in the wilderness of Tekoa; or Ezekiel living with the exiled Israelites in the midst of heathen Babylon. In every instance the hand of God was laid upon a man and he was commissioned to declare the Divine Will unto his nation and people. Like the great Apostle they could say: "Necessity is laid upon me; yea, woe is unto me, if I preach not the gospel!"

These prophets believed that they were directly called of God. When they stood forth to address the multitude they realized that they were speaking for or on behalf of God. They were God's spokesmen and so they prefaced their messages by declaring in accents of conviction: "Thus saith the Lord."

One of the most inspiring epochs in history is that of the prophets of Israel, these mighty men whose lips had been touched by the finger of God; whose hearts had been filled with the Divine fire; who lived in a day when the whole world was reeking of immorality, superstition, idolatry; when the weak were trampled under the feet of the strong; when the poor were despoiled by the rich; when religion itself had degenerated into licentious rites; when nation after nation was crashing to a destruction brought about by their own inherent corruption. Then, towering above the people of their day and generation, stood these spiritual giants proclaiming that Jehovah Eternal reigns, King of Kings and Lord of Lords, and that he demands righteousness not only of the lowly and the poor but also of the proud and the great. From a period more than seven hundred years before the birth of Christ we hear the inspiring words of one of them: "He hath showed thee, O man, what is good. And what doth the Lord require of thee but to do justly, to love mercy, and to walk humbly with thy God?"

The conception which St. Paul held of his own apostleship was not one whit lower than that of the prophets, for he said in one of his Epistles: "Paul, an apostle, not of men, neither by man, but by Jesus Christ, and God the Father, who raised him from the dead." He was commissioned not by man but by God himself. Every Protestant minister ought to entertain a view no less exalted of his calling.

Dr. John Henry Jowett never ceased to impress upon students for the ministry the necessity of cherishing in their souls the profound conviction that they were directly called of God. He said:

I hold that, before a man selects the Christian ministry as his vocation, he must have the assurance that the selection has been imperatively constrained by the Eternal God. The call of the Eternal must ring through the rooms of his soul as clearly as the sound of the morning bell rings through the valleys of Switzerland calling the peasants to early prayer and praise.

Any man who enters the ministry in such a spirit of dedication to the will of God will place his calling on so lofty a spiritual plane that no allurements can ever tempt him aside. He will say in the words of the Apostle: "For though I preach the gospel, I have nothing to glory of: for necessity is laid upon me; yea, woe is unto me, if I preach not the gospel!"

The question is sometimes asked in an atmosphere of withering cynicism whether, after all, this business of preaching is worth while. Some modern writers jest about the fact that hundreds of thousands of sermons are preached every Sunday on this continent. They declare that these messages are without visible result.

Exactly the same thing might be said of summer showers. The rain clouds pass and the sun comes out again. All traces of the shower disappear. The dust is blowing over the fields. But deep down in the soil little rootlets are eagerly drinking up the moisture that has fallen, and some day, because of the rain, there will be a bountiful harvest. That was the comforting message which God brought to the Prophet Isaiah: "Even as the rain cometh down, and the snow from heaven, and returneth not thither, but watereth the earth, and maketh it bring forth and bud, that it may give seed to the sower, and bread to the eater: So shall my word be that goeth forth out of my mouth: it shall not return unto me void, but it shall accomplish that which I please, and it shall prosper in the thing whereto I sent it."

There seldom has been a time in history when somebody was not declaring that the pulpit had lost its power. In the year 1882 a writer by the name of Mahaffy published a book with the title *The Decline of Modern Preaching.* When this book was coming off the press Joseph Parker, Dean Liddon, Charles Haddon Spurgeon, Alexander MacLaren, Henry Ward Beecher, and Phillips Brooks were in the full splendor of their power. It was the golden age of preaching in the nineteenth century, but the author of that book was too close to his time properly to estimate it.

That holds true for today. Ernest H. Jeffs declares that he disbelieves in the legend that "the royal epoch of the pulpit is behind us." "The Christian pulpit," he says, "was never more rich in preaching power than it is today and never more adequately equipped for the defence and advancement of the Faith in a day of doubt, questioning and wistful seeking."

No man can estimate the moral and spiritual uplift that is given to the lives of millions of men and women who, week by week, listen to the preaching of the Word. This country is a finer, cleaner, safer place in which to live because of the spiritual influence which radiates from our Christian churches. What is true of our day has been true of every century in history. The influence of Christian preachers has turned the course of history into new channels and has elevated the moral and spiritual life of mankind.

Let us look back across the centuries to some of the crucial epochs in the life of man and see what was accomplished by some of the pulpit giants of the Christian Church for the emancipation of humanity.

We go back to the middle of the fourth century of the Christian era. Julian the Apostate is on the throne of the Roman Empire. He is bitterly opposed to Christianity. Unceasingly he labors to make the whole world pagan. The rising tide of opposition threatens to engulf the Christian Church. Thousands of believers are fearful lest Christianity will not be able to weather the storm. In that dark hour God raises up a champion for the Faith. See him entering the pulpit of the cathedral at Alexandria! He is a little man, almost a dwarf in stature, with a pronounced stoop in his shoulders. His nose is aquiline and he wears an ugly, stubby beard. But when Bishop Athanasius rises to defend the Faith once delivered to the saints, the stoop goes out of his shoulders; he is no longer a dwarf but a giant in physical presence. He is a superman.

The Reverend Sylvester Horne has impressively summarized this preacher's life and work:

I like to read how that strange countenance was illumined to seraphic beauty by light of inward holiness and zeal for truth. Such was the mighty soul in the attenuated body of him who dared emperors and defied ecclesiastics, who was exiled again and again and again and yet again, who was as much at home in the caves of the Egyptian deserts as in the council-chamber of Nicæa or the palaces of Alexandria. No man was less depressed by defeat, or exalted by success. Yet the gorgeous annals of Constantine afford no parallel to the splendour of popular triumph, when Alexandria swept out beyond its walls to welcome back its banished preacher and bishop, the multitude of its people suggesting to an eye-witness the Nile overflowing its banks. Then came stepping along the sandy road out of the wilderness of his exile, the strange dwarf figure, with the beard whitened with toil and care, but the face still radiant, and the light in the eyes that told of the unconquerable soul.

This was the man who, in an age of Stygian darkness, held aloft the torch of Truth and, by his indomitable courage, drove back the invading forces of unbelief and moral chaos. Not until the last great Day of Reckoning will it be known how much the world owes to the preaching of Athanasius.

We move forward to the closing years of the fifteenth century. Again it was an hour of travail for the Christian Church. This time the peril was even more deadly because it came from within. Alexander VI, who occupied the Papal chair, was constantly involved in intrigue and violence. From the hierarchy at Rome down through all the rank and file of the clergy there was corruption and immorality. The ruling classes of Italy reveled in debaucheries. The masses were steeped in iniquity. Not a single voice in the Church was raised in protest, but a servile priesthood continued to cry "Peace," "Peace," where there was no peace.

One day into the pulpit of the little Church of San Marco in Florence walked a humble friar. He was without a friend in Italy. He had no authority and no influence with the powerful ruling classes. But Girolamo Savonarola possessed something of far greater value—the unshakable conviction that he had been called of Almighty God to denounce the sins of the Church and of the nation. Soon even the great Cathedral of Florence was not large enough to hold the multitudes that flocked out to hear him. With absolute fearlessness he arraigned the immoralities of the Papal court; the oppression of the nobles; the sins of the people; until within the space of a few years a miracle was witnessed—the conversion of a great city. A new King had come to Florence—even Jesus Christ—and he was enthroned in thousands of human hearts.

But the enemies of Savonarola plotted unceasingly to overthrow him. Pope Alexander Borgia was his unrelenting foe. At last the plotters succeeded. Savonarola was arrested; tortured for weeks; condemned to death; hanged on a gibbet in a public square and his body burned to ashes.

It is more than four hundred years since the dust of the Prophet of Florence was scattered to the four winds of the heavens, but his spirit still lives and continues to inspire the hearts of the people of Florence and of Italy today.

Finally, we move forward to the middle of the sixteenth century. The scene is set in the courtyard of the Castle of St. Andrews in Scotland. George Wishart, a great and holy man, is doomed to die. As the flames envelop his body hope dies in the hearts of Scotsmen and a pall of indescribable darkness settles over the land. But standing in the crowd that watches the valiant death of Wishart is a young priest whose soul is shaken by the spectacle. He hears a Voice calling him to take the place of the martyr who has perished. While he hesitates, a man of God visits him and leaves this message: "Refuse not this holy vocation as you look to avoid God's heavy displeasure." In that hour John Knox steps forth to battle for the spiritual emancipation of his beloved Scotland.

Not even the power and wiles of Mary, Queen of Scots, could break his resistance; and the Catholic Queen confessed that she feared his prayers "more than an army of an hundred thousand men."

Listen to Thomas Carlyle:

> In the history of Scotland I can find but one epoch. It contains nothing of world interest at all but this Reformation by Knox. . . . Scotch literature and thought, Scotch industry, James Watt, David Hume, Walter Scott, Robert Burns—I find John Knox acting in the heart's core of every one of these persons and phenomena. I find that without him they would not have been.

Carlyle was right. The greatest debt that Scotland owes to any man living or dead she owes to John Knox.

Here are but three men selected from the galaxy of prophets who have obeyed the command of Christ to go forth and preach, and whose inspiring leadership has played a mighty part in molding the course of human history not only in the age in which they lived but for all time. When, with these three, we think of Luther, Calvin, Whitefield, Wesley, Jonathan Edwards, Moody, Beecher, Brooks, and scores of others who kindled their torches at the same Beacon of Truth, then we have some little understanding of what preaching has done for the world.

It is easy enough to stand outside the Christian Church and criticize its mistakes and failures, for its record has not been perfect. It is easier to see from within how feebly it is witnessing for him who is its King and Head. Yet this Church has kept the lamp of truth alight in ages of darkness and has been an unceasing reminder to mankind of God's presence in the world. Its message has inspired men in every age to go forth to battle against injustice and oppression and all enslavement of man by man. It is the one institution that exists for the sole purpose of establishing in this bewildered and divided world the Kingdom of God. Let us then, who have pledged our allegiance to that Kingdom, be no longer mere camp followers but true soldiers of Christ, for we have entered upon a holy crusade in which there will be no armistice until the triumph of righteousness shall crown the strife of the ages and God's will shall be done in earth as it is now done in Heaven.